Contents

As we live in a rapidly changing society, exposure to and fluency in Science, Technology, Engineering, and Mathematics (STEM) ensures students will gain the skills they will need to succeed in the 21st century. It is essential that students gain practice in becoming good problem solvers, critical thinkers, innovators, inventors, and risk takers.

Teacher Tips

Encourage Topic Interest

Help students develop an understanding and appreciation of different STEM concepts by providing an area in the classroom to display topic-related non-fiction books, pictures, collections, and artifacts as a springboard for learning.

What I Think I Know / What I Would Like to Know Activity

Introduce each STEM unit by asking students what they think they know about the topic, and what they would like to know about the topic. Complete this activity as a whole-group brainstorming session, in cooperative small groups, or independently. Once students have had a chance to complete the questions, combine the information to create a class chart for display. Throughout the study, periodically update students' progress in accomplishing their goal of what they want to know, and validate what they think they know.

Vocabulary List

Keep track of new and content-related vocabulary on chart paper for students' reference. Encourage students to add words to the list. Classify the word list into the categories of nouns, verbs, and adjectives. In addition, have students create their own science dictionaries as part of their learning logs.

Learning Logs

Keeping a learning log is an effective way for students to organize thoughts and ideas about the STEM concepts presented and examined. Students' learning logs also provide insight on what follow-up activities are needed to review and to clarify concepts learned.

Learning logs can include the following types of entries:

- Teacher prompts
- Students' personal reflections
- Questions that arise
- Connections discovered
- Labeled diagrams and pictures
- Definitions for new vocabulary

Habitats

What Is a Habitat?

Habitats are places where living things live. Your habitat is your neighborhood.
A habitat provides what plants and animals need.

What Do Plants and Animals Need?

Here are some of the things that plants and animals need:

- **Food**—Plants and animals need food to live and to grow.
- **Water**—Living things need water to survive.
- **Air**—Plants and animals need air to stay alive.
- **Light**—Plants need light to grow. People and animals need light so they can see and to stay healthy.
- **Space**—Animals need space to hunt or gather food, find a mate, and raise a family. Plants need space, too. If too many plants grow too close together, they may not be able to get enough food from the soil or enough sunlight.

What Are Some Examples of Habitats?

Here are some examples of different habitats and the plants and animals that live in each one.

Habitat	Plants and Animals
Pond	Water plants, frogs, dragonflies, fish
Desert	Cactuses, coyote, scorpions, rattlesnakes
Rainforest	Trees, jaguars, sloths, birds

"Habitats"—Think About It!

1. Birds make homes called nests. Would it be correct to say that a bird's nest is its habitat? Why or why not?

_____

_____

_____

_____

_____

2. Could a mountain be a habitat for some plants and animals? Give reasons for your answer.

_____

_____

_____

_____

_____

3. Why is it important for animals to be able to find a mate in their habitat?

_____

_____

_____

_____

4. Think about what you know about beavers. Why is a lake or stream in a forest a good habitat for a beaver?

_____

_____

_____

_____

_____

Different Types of Habitats

There are many types of habitats around the world. Let us look at some types of habitats in North America.

Prairie

Prairies can be called grasslands because they are covered with grasses. Many types of flowers are found there, too. Trees and bushes do not grow well there.

Buffalo and pronghorn antelope eat prairie grasses. Wolves, coyotes, and foxes live in the prairie. They eat smaller animals, such as gophers and prairie dogs. Ground squirrels live on the ground and dig underground homes. Sparrows, hawks, and owls are birds that live in the prairie habitat.

City

Cities are habitats for humans, plants, and wild creatures. Ants dig homes in the sidewalk cracks. Birds hunt for worms on lawns. Mice live in people's houses. Trees and plants grow around homes. Weeds grow in ditches. Grasses and bushes grow in fields. Trees grow in city parks.

continued next page ☞

Wetland

Wetlands are found between water and dry land. Swamps and marshes are wetlands. This habitat may be very wet and muddy most of the time. Or the habitat may be underwater.

Trees, grasses, and bushes can grow in wetlands. Mosquitoes, dragonflies, fish, turtles, ducks, frogs, and snakes are just a few animals that can live in wetlands.

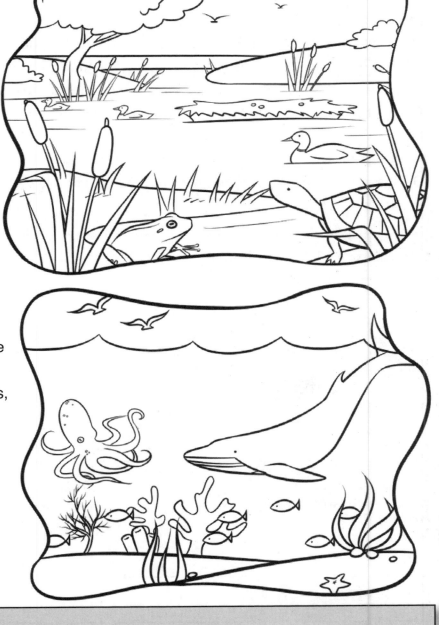

Ocean

Lots of animals live in the world's oceans. Whales and sharks are some of the larger ocean animals. Smaller animals include octopuses, sea jellies, and shrimp. Plankton are ocean creatures that are so tiny you need a microscope to see them. Brown, red, and green seaweed are plants that grow in an ocean habitat.

Birds live above the ocean. But they are also part of the ocean habitat because they hunt there.

Brain Stretch

Sometimes areas become what is called a critical habitat. This happens when a species is threatened, or is near extinction, and needs protection. Laws to prevent killing, removing, or bothering of the species protect the critical habitat. This effort helps the species survive and thrive.

Create a poster about a critical habitat near your community. Make sure to include information on what caused this area to become a critical habitat. Describe what is being done to help this area recover.

"Different Types of Habitats"—Think About It!

Read about the animals below. Then write in the chart which habitat (prairie, city, wetland, or ocean) you think each animal lives in. Give reasons for your answer.

- **Raccoons** tip over people's garbage cans and make a big mess as they look for food.
- **Coral** is beautiful to look at, but scuba divers have to be careful. Coral can be very sharp and cause a nasty cut.
- **Alligators** live in swampy areas where they hunt animals that live in water and on land.
- **Badgers** are fantastic diggers that hunt animals that live in underground homes, such as ground squirrels.

1. Raccoon	Habitat:
Why I think so:	
2. Coral	Habitat:
Why I think so:	
3. Alligator	Habitat:
Why I think so:	
4. Badger	Habitat:
Why I think so:	

Brain Stretch

On a separate piece of paper, draw and label your own habitat. What types of animals and plants will live in your habitat? What type of climate will it have? How much precipitation?

Animal Adaptations

Over very long periods of time—thousands or millions of years—animals can change so that they are better able to survive. These changes are called adaptations.

Feathers Are Not Just for Flying

The feathers you find on birds' wings help them to fly. But birds have feathers all over their body, so what are these feathers for? Feathers help to keep birds warm. Without feathers, birds might die if the weather gets too cold. Over time, birds developed feathers as an adaptation that helped them to survive in habitats where the weather gets cold.

Reach for the Top

Humans do not have a long neck. Our neck helps us turn our head left and right and up and down—we do not need a long neck to do that. Now think of a giraffe's neck. Why would a giraffe need such a long neck?

Giraffes feed on leaves that grow on tall trees. If a giraffe could reach only the lowest leaves on a tree, it might have trouble finding enough food to survive. But with such a long neck, a giraffe can reach even the leaves that grow near the top of a tree. The giraffe's long neck is an adaptation that helps it to survive.

The Tale of a Tail

Beavers are famous for their wide, flat tails. This adaptation helps beavers in several ways.

The shape of beavers' tails helps them steer in the water. But that is not all their tails do. Beavers' tails help them balance when moving a heavy branch to build a home.

Their tails are also alarms. They slap their tails on the water to warn others that danger is near.

continued next page 👉

Open Wide…Very Wide!

How can a snake swallow an animal bigger than its own head? This adaptation lets snakes hunt larger animals, making it easier for snakes to survive.

A snake's jaws work differently than human jaws. A snake's top and bottom jaws can spread wide apart. This lets the mouth stretch to swallow a nice, big meal.

Snakes have another adaptation that helps them swallow food. Their teeth point to the back of their mouths. This means that a meal will not get stuck on the teeth as the snake swallows it. It also means a meal will not be able to escape once it is caught.

"Animal Adaptations"—Think About It!

1. Using information from the text and your own ideas, write about why adaptations are important for an animal's survival.

_____

_____

_____

_____

_____

_____

_____

_____

_____

_____

"Animal Adaptations"—Think About It! (continued)

For each animal below, write one adaptation that helps the animal swim, hunt, or hide.

2. Swimming

Duck _____

Fish _____

Seal _____

3. Hunting

Owl _____

Rattlesnake _____

Shark _____

4. Hiding

Polar bear _____

Chameleon _____

Turtle _____

Humans and Habitats

How do humans affect natural habitats?

More People

The population of Earth is growing. More space is needed for things such as homes, hospitals, schools, stores, and factories. Natural habitats are destroyed by building on them.

Think of the plants and animals that might live in a habitat. They might disappear from the area forever.

More Pollution

Humans create pollution. When there are more people, there is more pollution. Here are some examples:

- Factories put smoke into the air. Chemicals in the smoke are harmful to plants and animals.
- Factories dump liquid waste into lakes and rivers. Chemicals in the waste poison life in lakes and rivers. Dangerous chemicals build up inside a fish's body. If you eat the fish, those chemicals go into *your* body.
- People pour dangerous chemicals down drains. These chemicals might end up in lakes and rivers. They might end up in our drinking water. Many people do not realize that things such as paint, old medicines, and cleaning products contain harmful chemicals.

More Hope for the Future

Today, more and more people realize that it is important to protect habitats. More people are trying to save natural habitats. Here are some of the things people are doing:

- Recycling wood and paper products. This means fewer trees need to be cut down.
- Finding ways for factories to produce less pollution.
- Taking dangerous liquids to hazardous waste facilities.

"Humans and Habitats"—Think About It!

The town of Fieldstone is growing quickly and needs more space to build houses. At the edge of the town, there is a large forest. There are plans to cut down the forest to build houses. How might different people feel about this plan?

1. You are a developer whose job is building houses. If you cannot find space to build houses, your business might not survive. How do you feel about the plan? Why?

_____

_____

_____

_____

2. You are an ecologist who studies natural habitats. You work to find ways to protect the plants and animals that live in forests. How do you feel about the plan? Why?

_____

_____

_____

_____

3. Your family has grown too large for the small apartment where you live. There are not many houses for sale in Fieldstone, and most of them are too expensive. The new houses that would be built on the forest land would be big enough for your family and not too expensive. How do you feel about the plan? Why?

_____

_____

_____

_____

Role Play

Set up a town council meeting and enact what might happen when the issue is discussed. Prepare for the roles of council member, developer, citizen, and ecologist.

Habitat Communities

What Is a Community?

The word community can mean a group of people together in one place. Your neighborhood is a community. The people in your neighborhood all live in the same area.

Depending on Each Other

People in communities depend on one another. Think of your school community. Students need teachers to teach them. Teachers need students to teach. Principals make sure their schools run smoothly. Principals need everyone else to help. The people in your school community need each other.

Plants and animals make communities, too.

Habitat Communities

A habitat community is made up of all the plants and animals that live in a particular habitat. They depend on each other.

Animals in a community need the plants. Plants provide some animals with food. They provide places to hide. They also provide homes.

Plants in a community need the animals. Animal droppings fertilize the soil. This helps plants grow. Bees move pollen between flowers while they eat. This helps plants produce seeds and fruit.

Some animals depend on other animals for food. For example, mice provide food for owls.

Why Habitat Communities Are Important

What if all the trees disappeared from a habitat? Plants would not have shady places to grow. Birds' nests would be on the ground. Predators could eat birds' eggs.

Imagine that all the mice disappeared. Animals that eat mice might not find enough food to survive.

Every living thing in a habitat community depends on each other. They help each other to survive. They may not survive without each other.

"Habitat Communities"—Think About It!

1. How is a habitat community similar to your school community?

_____

_____

_____

_____

2. Which is more important in a habitat community—animals or plants? Or are animals and plants equally important? Give reasons for your answer.

_____

_____

_____

_____

3. Choose a habitat. Sketch a scene that shows at least two examples of how the animals and plants in a habitat community depend on each other. Label the habitat you sketched.

Habitat: _____

Food Chains

It Is All About Energy

All living things need energy. Plants need energy to grow. Animals and humans need energy to grow into adults. They also need energy to move and to keep their bodies working properly. How do plants, animals, and humans get energy?

Plants need sunlight because they get energy from the Sun. Some animals eat plants to get energy. They take in the energy that the plant got from sunlight.

When an animal eats a plant, the energy in the plant goes into the animal. Giraffes get energy from the leaves and twigs they eat. If a lion eats the giraffe, the lion takes in the energy that the giraffe got from its food.

Humans and some animals eat plants and animals. They get energy from both types of food. Sunlight is a form of energy. The diagram below shows how energy moves between living things. This energy moves in the form of food.

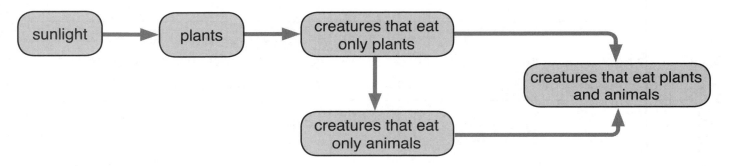

Who Eats What?

A food chain shows how the energy that starts out as sunlight moves from one living thing to another. For example,

1. Grass gets energy from sunlight.
2. Grasshoppers eat grass.
3. Frogs eat grasshoppers.
4. Snakes eat frogs.
5. Owls eat snakes.

We can make a diagram to show a food chain. Start at "sunlight" and follow the food chain. Each time you see an arrow, say "gives energy to."

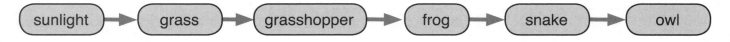

"Food Chains"—Think About It!

1. Why is sunlight so important in a food chain?

_____

_____

_____

2. Look at the food chain at the bottom of page 14. What would happen if all the grasshoppers disappeared? Why?

_____

_____

_____

3. Use the information below to complete the food chain. Write each bold word in the correct place on the food chain.

- A **rabbit** eats leaves from some plants.
- A **plant** gets energy from sunlight.
- A **fox** eats rabbits.
- **Sunlight** is a form of energy.

4. Read about Arctic creatures. Then use the bold words to complete the food chain.

Shrimp live in the cold Arctic water. They eat tiny living things called algae. Many types of algae are tiny plants. Polar bears go out on the ice to hunt for seals. Seals eat lots of fish. The fish do not mind the cold. They spend their time hunting for food such as shrimp.

algae   **polar bear**   **shrimp**   **seal**   **sunlight**   **fish**

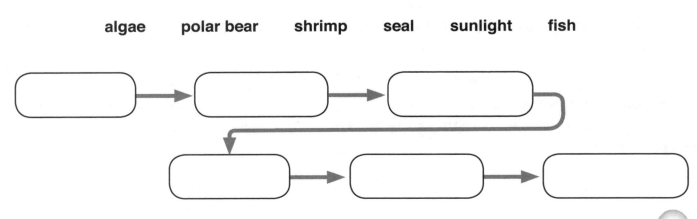

Producers, Consumers, and Decomposers

Living things can be grouped into three categories:

- *Producers*—Plants are called producers because they use energy from sunlight to make the food they need. (*Produce* means to make or create.)
- *Consumers*—Animals are consumers. They cannot make their own food the way plants can. Instead, animals eat plants or other animals. Some animals eat both. (*Consume* means to eat.)
- *Decomposers*—Some living things break down dead plants and animals into very tiny pieces. These pieces go into the soil, where plants absorb them and—with the help of sunlight— make the food they need. Some examples of decomposers are mushrooms, bacteria, and earthworms. (*Decompose* means to break down.)

The living things in a food chain are all producers or consumers. Here is an example:

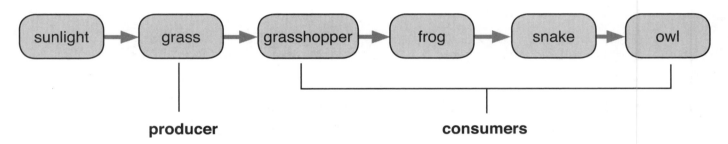

What about sunlight? Sunlight is not a living thing, so it is not a producer, consumer, or decomposer.

Yuck! Dead Things!

You might not like dead plants and animals, but decomposers sure do. That is a good thing. Decomposers play an important role in a food chain.

Look at the food chain above. When any of the consumers die, parts of their bodies may be eaten by scavengers. (*Scavengers* are animals that eat dead animals). The scavengers may leave behind some tasty bits that they were not able to eat. Then the decomposers move in to finish the job. They break down some parts of an animal's body that scavengers did not eat.

Remember that some decomposers break down dead plants. When any living thing dies, decomposers help turn it into tiny pieces that living plants can use to make food. You can think of decomposers as living things that recycle dead plants and animals into something useful for plants.

"Producers, Consumers, and Decomposers"—Think About It!

1. Circle the living thing below that is **not** a producer. Then explain your choice.

tulip   tree   dandelion   butterfly   carrot

A _____ is not a producer because _____

_____

_____

2. Why are decomposers important in a food chain?

_____

_____

_____

_____

3. Label the producers and consumers in this food chain. Use **P** for producer and **C** for consumer.

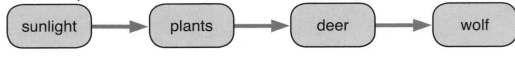

sunlight → plants → deer → wolf

_____   _____   _____   _____

4. Why would living animals have a difficult time if all the decomposers disappeared?

_____

_____

_____

_____

5. Write **True** or **False** beside each sentence.

a) Only animals that eat other animals are consumers. _____

b) Plants need only sunlight and water to survive. _____

What Is for Dinner?

Animals are called consumers because they must find food to eat. They cannot make their own food. Consumers can be put in three groups, based on the food they eat.

Carnivores

A carnivore is an animal that eats other animals. Many types of animals are carnivores. Here are a few examples:

- Lions eat large mammals such as zebras, buffalo, and antelopes.
- Polar bears' favorite food is seals. They eat other animals, too.
- Frogs eat insects, worms, and snails.
- Dragonflies eat other insects.

Herbivores

Herbivores are animals that eat plants. Some herbivores eat only grass and leaves. Other herbivores eat flowers, fruits, seeds, or even wood. Here are examples of herbivores:

- Sheep eat leaves and grass.
- Elephants eat leaves, twigs, and bark. They eat fruits, seeds, and flowers, too.
- Bees eat the pollen and nectar they find in flowers.
- Parrots eat fruits and nuts.

Omnivores

An omnivore is an animal that eats plants and animals. Which of these omnivores have you seen?

- Black bears mostly eat leaves, nuts, and berries. They will also eat animals such as ants, bees, salmon, and trout.
- Robins eat worms, insects, and berries.
- Skunks eat animals such as insects, worms, and frogs. Berries, roots, leaves, and nuts are also part of a skunk's diet.
- Snapping turtles eat a variety of plants. They will also eat small fish, frogs, insects, and snakes.

Word Stretch

The words *carnivore, herbivore,* and *omnivore* are all nouns. Each of these words has an adjective form: *carnivorous, herbivorous,* and *omnivorous.*

A **carnivorous** animal is called a **carnivore.** A **herbivorous** animal is called an **herbivore.** An **omnivorous** animal is called an **omnivore.**

"What Is for Dinner?"—Think About It!

1. Write each animal where it belongs in the Venn diagram. Using your knowledge, add more animals that fit each description.

butterfly   chimpanzee   deer   dolphin   giraffe   pig   raccoon   shark   snake

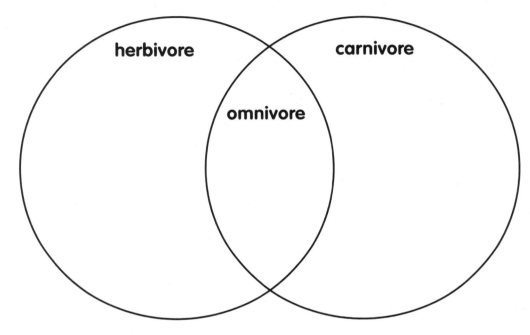

2. What type of consumers are humans? Write "humans" where it belongs in the diagram above.

3. Choose from the words below to fill in the blanks. Think about whether you need to use a noun or an adjective.

carnivore   carnivorous   herbivore   herbivorous   omnivore   omnivorous

a) _____ animals often have sharp claws that help them to hunt

other animals.

b) The kangaroo is an _____ whose favorite food is grass.

c) The red fox is _____ because it eats birds and small

mammals, along with fruits, berries, and grass.

d) Like many _____ animals, porcupines eat twigs and buds from

trees, as well as leaves.

Natural Habitats and Humans

What Is a Natural Habitat?

A natural habitat is not made by humans. Examples include deserts, forests, rivers, oceans, and lakes.

Cities are habitats for many living things. Plants, birds, insects, and squirrels live in cities. Humans create cities. Cities are not natural habitats.

How Do Humans Depend on Natural Habitats?

Humans depend on natural habitats. Look at some ways natural habitats help us.

Wood and paper products: These are made from trees that grow in forests. Wood is used to build homes and furniture. Wood is also used to make paper, paper towels, and tissues.

Oxygen: Oxygen is an important part of the air we breathe. Humans can not survive without it. Plants and trees make oxygen. We need forests to make oxygen.

Food: Most of our food comes from farms. In some places, people get food from nature. They hunt animals. They gather plants from nature.

Flood control: When lots of rain falls quickly, floods can happen. Rainwater flows into rivers and streams. These can overflow into the land around them. Floods can damage people's homes. They can destroy the crops in farmers' fields. Wetlands, such as marshes and swamps, help control floods. Wetland plants act like sponges, absorbing much of the water. Without wetlands, floods would be worse.

Medicine: Many ingredients for medicine come from plants. Many of those plants are found only in natural habitats such as forests. For example, willow bark relieves pain. It is a chemical used in Aspirin®. New plants are being discovered. Some may be used to make medicines.

Recreation: Natural habitats are fun. Whitewater rafting happens on a river. Downhill skiing needs a mountain. Lakes are great for swimming, boating, and waterskiing. Lots of people enjoy hiking or camping in forests. These activities need natural habitats.

Brain Stretch

Using information from the text and your own ideas, write about how natural habitats are helpful to you and your community.

"Natural Habitats and Humans"—Think About It!

1. Is a farm a natural habitat? Why or why not? _____

_____

_____

_____

_____

2. How does recycling paper products help to save forest habitats? _____

_____

_____

_____

3. Draw a picture showing one thing that you like to do in a natural habitat. Or, show an activity you have not done but would like to try. Label the habitat shown in your picture.

Habitat: _____

Generalist and Specialist Animals and Plants

Some animals can live in different habitats. For example, raccoons can live in cities, swamps, or forests. Raccoons do not have special needs. They can eat many foods and can make homes in many places. A raccoon home can be in a hollow tree, a cave, or the attic of a house.

Animals that can live in different habitats are called generalist animals.

Animals that have special needs are called specialist animals. They can live only in habitats that meet their special needs. For example, the giant panda eats only bamboo plants. It can only live where bamboo grows.

There are also generalist plants and specialist plants. A generalist plant can live in many different habitats. A dandelion does not have special needs. Dandelions can live in forests, rocky hillsides, and gardens. The dandelion is a generalist plant.

A specialist plant can live only in certain places. A cactus is a specialist plant. It will die if it is in extreme cold for too long or if it gets too much water.

Think About It!

1. Circle the correct word in bold.

a) The koala eats only eucalyptus leaves. It is a **(generalist, specialist)** animal.

b) Omnivores can eat plants and animals. Most omnivores are **(generalist, specialist)** animals.

2. If a habitat changes, which types of plants and animals will be affected most—generalist or specialist? Explain why you think so.

_____

_____

_____

_____

_____

_____

Habitat Word Search

Complete the sentences, then find the correct answers in the word search.

1. The area where a plant or animal lives is called its _____.

2. An _____ is a change that helps an animal survive.
   The change happens over a long time.

3. All the plants and animals that live in a habitat are called a habitat _____.

4. A food _____ shows how energy moves from one living thing to another.

5. A _____ breaks down dead plants and animals.

6. A _____ is an animal that eats other animals.

Look also for these words related to the topic of habitats:

desert	humans	pollution	specialist
energy	ocean	pond	survive
food	plant	producer	tree

A	C	O	M	M	U	N	I	T	Y	S	R	L
N	D	E	S	E	R	T	F	A	N	P	O	A
O	E	A	C	N	A	E	I	T	R	E	E	E
I	C	Y	P	O	C	E	N	I	E	C	A	R
T	O	D	U	T	H	G	A	B	N	I	H	O
U	M	I	P	L	A	N	T	A	E	A	U	V
L	P	O	N	D	I	T	E	H	R	L	M	I
L	O	C	E	A	N	T	I	F	G	I	A	N
O	S	U	R	V	I	V	E	O	Y	S	N	R
P	E	M	A	T	G	Y	Q	O	N	T	S	A
P	R	O	D	U	C	E	R	D	E	D	A	C

What Is a Pulley?

Machines make our lives easier. They let us do tasks with much less effort. For example, think of an elevator. To use an elevator, just step in and push a button. Step off when you reach your floor. Now think of using the stairs. Climbing stairs takes much more effort, and takes more time, too.

Machines can save both time and effort. Not all machines are complicated. Some are very simple. A wheel is a simple machine. Wheels make it easier to move heavy loads. Small wheels on heavy furniture makes the furniture easier to move.

A pulley is a simple machine that uses a wheel that has a groove in it. A rope or cable fits into the groove. The wheel helps the rope move.

A pulley can be placed above a heavy object that you want to lift. You pull down on the rope to lift the object. It is easier to lift an object by pulling down than by pulling up. When you pull down, you can use the weight of your body to help you.

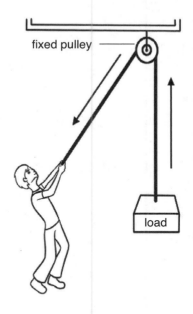

The object a pulley lifts is called the load.

Fixed Pulleys

The pulley shown here is a fixed pulley. It stays in one place.

Your muscles apply force to move something. When you lift an object without using a machine, the direction of force is up. Using a fixed pulley changes the direction of the force. The diagram shows a person pulling down on the rope. The direction of the force is down, but the object is lifted up.

Movable Pulleys

A movable pulley changes position. It is not attached to a structure. The movable pulley shown here moves up when the rope is pulled. It takes less force to lift an object with a movable pulley than with a fixed pulley.

A compound pulley is made up of a two or more pulleys. The diagram shows a compound pulley.

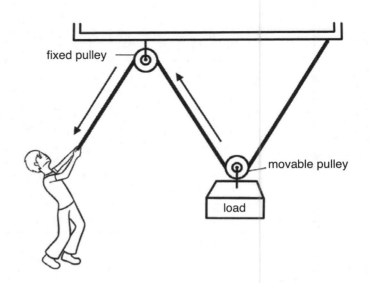

A compound pulley. As the rope is pulled down, the movable pulley moves up.

"What Is a Pulley?"—Think About It!

1. Think about one movable pulley attached to a load. What direction do you need to pull the rope to lift the load?

_____

_____

_____

_____

2. Look at the diagram at the bottom of page 24. What direction do you need to pull the rope to lift the load?

_____

_____

_____

_____

3. What are two advantages of using a compound pulley like the one shown on page 24?

_____

_____

_____

_____

4. Describe a way you use a simple machine in your daily life.

_____

_____

_____

_____

_____

_____

Experiment: Make a Simple Pulley

In this experiment, you will find out if a pulley makes it easier to lift a load. A broom handle will act as the pulley.

What You Need

- A plastic jug with a screw-on lid, half-full of water
- A broom handle
- A piece of thin rope or very strong string, 39 in (100 cm) long
- Two chairs with seats the same height
- Duct tape
- A ruler

What You Do

1. Tie the rope to the handle of the jug.
2. Place the two chairs 20 in (50 cm) apart.
3. Use the duct tape to attach the broom handle to the chair seats.
4. Have a partner hold a ruler on the floor beside the jug. Stand the ruler up, as shown. Pull the rope to lift the jug 12 in (30 cm).
5. Put the jug under the broom handle and place the rope over the broom handle as shown. Pull the rope down to lift the jug 12 in (30 cm).
6. Decide which method of lifting the jug was easier.

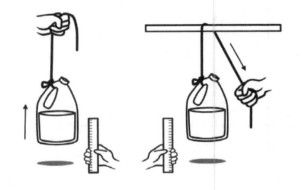

Think About It!

1. The rope and broom handle function as a pulley. Is it a fixed or movable pulley? Why do you think so?

_____

_____

_____

_____

Experiment: Make a Movable Pulley

Try this experiment to see how a movable pulley works.

What You Need

- A metal spoon
- A large, sturdy paper clip
- Two pieces of string, one 12 in (30 cm) long and one 39 in (100 cm) long
- Masking tape
- A table

What You Do

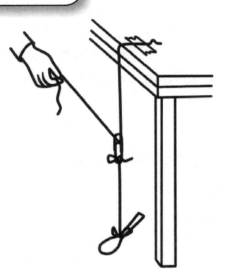

1. Tie one end of the 12 in (30 cm) piece of string to the spoon. Tie the other end to the paper clip.
2. Tape one end of the 39 in (100 cm) piece of string to the edge of the tabletop. Run the other end of the string through the paper clip.
3. Pull the string to lift the spoon.
4. Notice what happens to the position of the paper clip as you pull the string.

Think About It!

1. What happened to the position of the paper clip as you pulled the string? Why?

_____

_____

_____

2. Imagine you wanted to lift a heavy book. What would you change in this experiment? Why?

_____

_____

_____

_____

What Is a Gear?

A gear is a wheel that has teeth around its edge. The teeth of one gear fit into the spaces between the teeth on the other gear.

When one gear turns, it makes the other gear turn. The second gear wheel will turn in the opposite direction to the first gear. See if you can picture this in your mind as you look at the diagrams.

When you connect several gears in a row, you are creating a gear train. When a force makes any one gear turn, all the gears in the gear train will turn. Each gear turns in the opposite direction to the gears beside it.

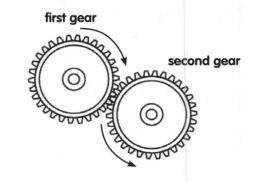

first gear
second gear

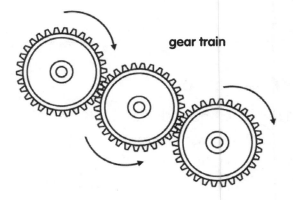

gear train

Gears and Speed

When we talk about speed, we are talking about how far something moves in a set period of time. Gears can be used to change the speed of movement. When one gear is connected to a gear of a different size, the two gear wheels will move at different speeds.

Look at the two gear wheels shown. When the large gear wheel moves, it makes the smaller gear move. The smaller gear will move faster than the larger gear. Why does this happen?

One tooth on the large gear will move one tooth on the small gear. When the large gear makes one half of a turn, the small gear will make a full turn. The small gear moves twice as fast as the large gear because it has half as many teeth.

By using gears that are two different sizes, we can change the speed of the motion.

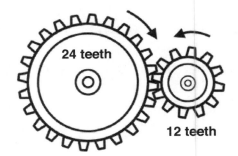

spur gears of different sizes

24 teeth

12 teeth

"What Is a Gear?"—Think About It!

1. Look at the gear trains shown below. Draw an arrow to show the direction each gear will turn.

a) Five spur gears in a row, all the same size. An arrow shows that the middle gear is turning counter-clockwise.

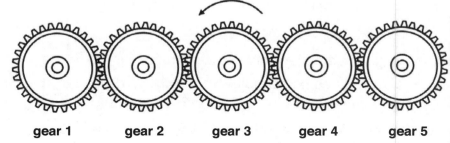

gear 1   gear 2   gear 3   gear 4   gear 5

b) Three gear wheels in a row, with a fourth gear directly under the middle gear. All gear wheels are the same size. An arrow shows that the fourth gear is turning clockwise.

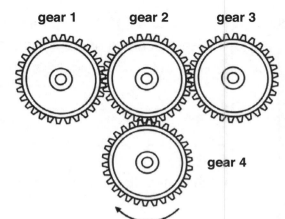

gear 1   gear 2   gear 3

gear 4

2. In this gear train, a small gear makes a larger gear turn. Will the larger gear turn faster or slower than the small gear? Why?

_____

_____

_____

_____

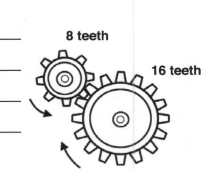

8 teeth

16 teeth

3. Look at the diagram at the bottom of page 28. When the small gear makes three turns, how many turns will the large gear make? How do you know?

_____

_____

_____

_____

Pulleys and Gears in Daily Life

Machines can make work easier. Many machines use pulleys and gears. Taking an elevator is easier than climbing stairs. Pulleys and gears make an elevator work.

Clothes dryers use pulleys and gears to tumble clothes. Clotheslines use sunshine and wind to dry clothes. Clotheslines use pulleys, too. The pulleys on a clothesline let you stand in one place and move the line.

Cars, buses, and bicycles move people from place to place. Those machines use pulleys and gears. Many machines at home use pulleys and gears, too.

Think About It!

1. Look at the clothesline with pulleys. Why are two pulleys required?

_____

_____

_____

2. Pulleys and gears help to make things move. Why does a clothes dryer need pulleys and gears?

_____

_____

_____

3. Flagpoles use one or two pulleys to raise and lower a flag. Pulleys are useful for lifting heavy objects. A flag is not heavy. Why are pulleys used on flagpoles?

_____

_____

_____

Opposite Directions

Pulleys and gears can change the direction of motion. In a gear train, several gears contact each other. Each gear moves in the opposite direction of its neighbors.

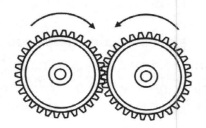

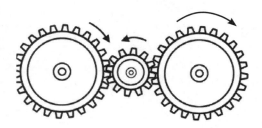

Imagine a machine that uses gears like the ones above. But there is a problem—the two gears need to move in the same direction. How could you do that?

This problem is not difficult to solve. Simply insert a gear in the middle.

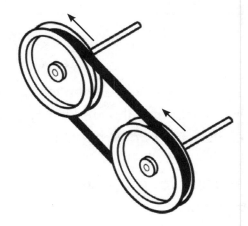

You can connect two pulleys with a belt or chain. This makes a drive system. Both pulleys will move in the same direction.

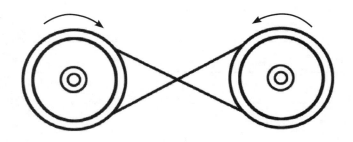

If the belt is crossed between two pulleys, the pulleys will move in opposite directions.

"Opposite Directions"—Think About It!

1. In this drive system, a belt connects four pulleys.
The direction pulley A turns is shown.
Notice that the belt is crossed beside pulley B.

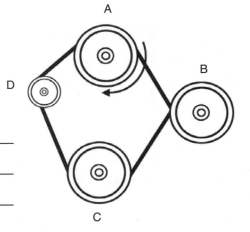

a) Will pulley B turn clockwise or counter-clockwise? Why?

_____

_____

_____

_____

b) In which direction will pulley D turn? Clockwise or counter-clockwise? Why?

_____

_____

_____

2. Lydia and Max were experimenting with gears. They wondered what would happen if they made a gear train in a circle shape. But their gear train would not turn!

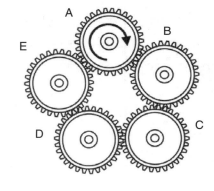

a) What is the problem? (**Hint:** Mark the direction that each gear turns.)

_____

_____

_____

_____

b) What change could solve the problem?

_____

_____

_____

Changing Direction: Bevel Gears

A spur gear has a wheel with teeth around the outside. Spur gears work when gears are in a straight line. They can be horizontal or vertical. A can opener uses a spur gear.

horizontal motion

Some gears can change the direction of the motion. A bevel gear can turn a vertical motion into a horizontal motion.

The teeth on a bevel gear are beveled (slanted). This lets the teeth of two bevel gears fit together at an angle. The bottom gear has a horizontal motion. The top gear has a vertical motion.

vertical motion

The pot below uses a bevel gear. A person turns the handle vertically. The gears change the direction of motion to horizontal. That makes the paddle inside turn horizontally.

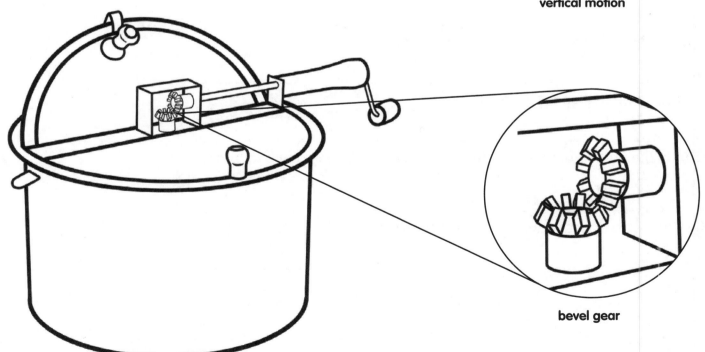

bevel gear

continued next page 👉

"Changing Direction: Bevel Gears"—Think About It!

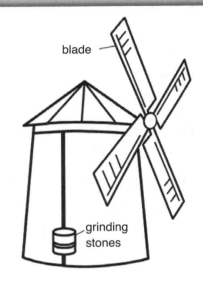

blade

Windmills were once used to grind grain. Wind turned the blades. This turned a bar attached to a stone. Below that stone was another stone that did not move. The grain was placed between the stones. The heavy, turning stone crushed the grain.

grinding stones

Use the diagram above to answer the questions.

1. What force makes the windmill blades turn?

_____

2. Do the blades turn horizontally or vertically?

_____

3. Does the grinding stone turn horizontally or vertically?

_____

4. What force makes the stone turn?

_____

5. To make the top grinding stone turn, the windmill uses gears to turn

_____ motion into _____ motion.

6. Which type of gears are used in a windmill: spur gears or bevel gears? Why?

_____

_____

_____

_____

_____

Changing Direction: Worm Gears

Spur gears and bevel gears have several teeth. A worm gear has just one tooth. The tooth spirals along a rod that looks a lot like the thread on a screw. A worm gear can be used to make a spur gear turn.

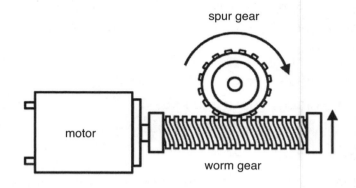

spur gear

motor

worm gear

The diagram shows a motor turning a worm gear. The worm gear makes the spur gear turn. The two gears turn at a right angle to each other. (Notice the direction arrows.)

You can use a worm gear to make a spur gear turn, but you cannot use a spur gear to make a worm gear turn. Friction will stop the gears from turning.

This toy clock helps children learn to tell time. By turning the knob at the top, you make the clock's hands move to show any time. This toy uses a worm gear and spur gears.

Think About It!

1. What supplies the force to move the clock's hands?

_____

2. Does the knob at the top turn a spur gear or a worm gear? How do you know?

_____

_____

3. Could bevel gears be used instead of the worm gear? Explain your thinking.

_____

_____

4. Does force change direction in this toy? Tell what happens.

_____

_____

Changing Direction: Rack and Pinion

What is a rack and pinion system? The pinion is a spur gear. The rack is a flat, straight piece with spurs. The teeth on the spur gear fit between the teeth on the rack.

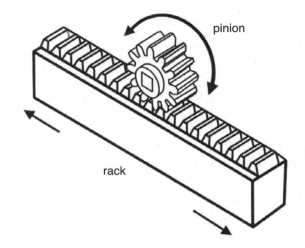

The pinion moves clockwise *and* counter-clockwise to move the rack back and forth. The circular motion of the pinion is turned into the back-and-forth motion of the rack.

Some buckles use a rack and pinion. You might have one on your skates or other sports equipment. A handle moves the pinion. The pinion moves the rack. The rack pulls the buckle tight.

Think About It!

Use the diagram above to answer the questions.

1. How can a pinion tighten a buckle?

_____

_____

2. In a buckle, what force makes the gears move?

_____

3. Turning a handle can open a window. The turning pushes a bar. The bar moves the window. Which part is the pinion? Which part is the rack?

_____

_____

4. Imagine moving the rack back and forth. What would happen to the pinion?

_____

_____

Bicycle Gears

Bicycles have two sets of gears. The front gears are connected to the pedals. The back gears are connected to the rear wheel. The bicycle chain connects the front gears to the back gears. Changing gears changes the amount of force needed to move forward.

High Speed, Low Speed

Notice the different sizes of the gears at the back. The smaller gears are the high speed. The larger gears are the low speed.

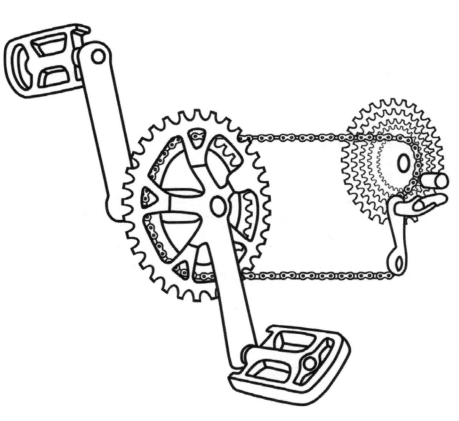

In low speed, the chain is on the largest gear. This largest gear moves the back wheel about as fast as you move the pedals. The bicycle moves more slowly than in higher speed, but pedaling is easier.

When the bike is in high speed, the chain moves onto the smallest gear. The wheel moves many times each time the pedal turns. The bicycle moves more quickly, but you have to pedal harder.

Input and Output

Machines need a force to make them work. The input component of a machine is the part that makes the other parts move. On a bicycle, the pedals are the input component.

The output component of a machine is the last part that moves. Bicycle pedals make the rear wheel move. The rear wheel is the output component.

"Bicycle Gears"—Think About It!

1. Which gear makes riding uphill easier—the smallest gear or the largest? Why?

_____

_____

_____

2. Which gear is better for racing on a flat road—the smallest or the largest? Why?

_____

_____

_____

3. Do bicycle gears change the direction of motion? Do they change the amount of force needed? Explain your answer.

_____

_____

_____

4. A tricycle does not use gears or a chain. The pedals move the front wheel. Which is the output component—the front wheel or the back wheels? How do you know?

_____

_____

_____

_____

_____

_____

Pulleys at Work: Conveyor Belt

Gears and pulleys are all around. The conveyor belt at the checkout counter uses gears and pulleys. Electricity turns the gear at one end. The belt moves the pulley at the other end.

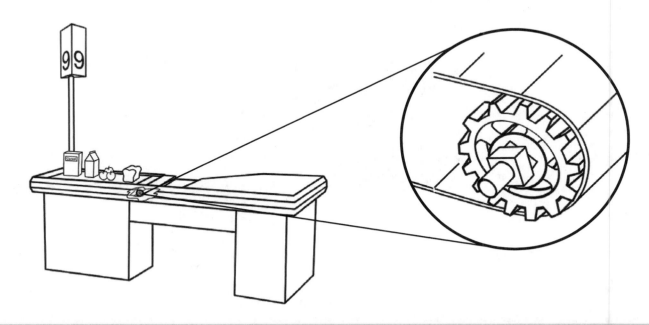

Think About It!

1. Machines save us time and effort. Explain how a conveyor belt saves both time and effort.

_____

_____

_____

_____

2. The gear at one end of the conveyor belt turns clockwise. Which direction does the pulley at the other end turn—clockwise or counter-clockwise? Explain why.

_____

_____

_____

_____

_____

Gears at Work: Pencil Sharpener

This diagram shows the inside of a pencil sharpener. Turning the handle turns gears that turn the cutting wheels. The cutting wheels sharpen the pencil.

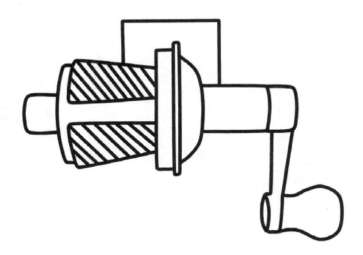

Think About It!

1. Which part is the input component of this pencil sharpener? Which part is the output component? Explain how you know.

_____

_____

_____

_____

_____

2. Does this pencil sharpener turn horizontal motion into vertical motion? Explain your thinking.

_____

_____

_____

_____

_____

Pulleys and Gears Riddles

1. I am the name for any object that you lift with a pulley.

   I am the _____.

2. I am the type of pulley that changes position.

   What type of pulley am I? _____

3. I am the part of a spur gear that makes other gears turn.

   I am the _____.

4. I can make a spur gear turn, but a spur gear cannot turn me!

   What type of gear am I? _____

5. My buddy and I are gears with slanted teeth. When we work together, we can

   turn vertical movement into horizontal movement. What type of gears are we?

   _____

6. My partner and I are gears that can tighten a buckle. We turn circular motion into

   back-and-forth motion. What are our names? _____

7. I make the front gear on a bicycle turn the back wheel.

   What am I? _____

8. We are the input component on a bicycle. Without us, you will not go anywhere!

   What are we? _____

9. Unscramble the secret message below.

   LEPSULY DAN AGERS KEAM SHGNTI VOEM!

   _____

Two Ways to Save Energy

Machines make our lives easier, but machines need energy. A motorcycle needs to burn gas, a dishwasher needs electricity, and a bicycle needs muscle power. These are all types of energy.

Saving energy is important because that saves money and makes less pollution. But we need machines. Machines help us travel far and quickly. Machines help build roads and clean our clothes. A machine can do the work of many strong people.

There are many ways to save energy. You could use more efficient machines, or you could use muscle energy instead. Muscles do not pollute.

Some people do both. Think of family with six people. They have a lot of laundry to do. They could use an efficient clothes dryer to save energy. And they can use a clothesline when it is sunny.

Brain Stretch

On a separate piece of paper, design a poster that lists tips for how to save energy. Use this checklist to check over your final product.

❑ My poster is organized.
❑ Each tip is easy to read and understand.
❑ My poster has pictures or graphics.
❑ I checked the spelling.
❑ I checked the punctuation.

"Two Ways to Save Energy"—Think About It!

Think about each story. Think about each person's needs. How could less energy be used?

1. Mrs. Petrof drives to work. There is a bus stop nearby. The bus does not come often. It is too cold to wait outside in winter. How could she save energy?

_____

_____

_____

_____

_____

_____

_____

2. Mr. Chan manages an apartment building. It has four floors. He wants people to save energy. A sign by the elevator says "Please use the stairs." Mrs. Chadwich uses a wheelchair. She has to use the elevator. She feels bad that she cannot save energy. Write another sign that will not hurt her feelings.

_____

_____

_____

_____

_____

_____

_____

_____

_____

_____

Sources of Light

Where does light come from?
Light comes from two sources.
One source is natural light. This
means that the light comes from
nature. Light from the Sun is natural
because the Sun makes its own
light.

natural light

artificial light

The other source of light is artificial.
This means that the light is made
by people. Lightbulbs are artificial
because people made them.

Most light sources give off their own light. Our Sun and other stars
make their own light. Candles and lightbulbs also make their own
light. But what about the Moon? We can see light from the Moon, but
it does not make light because it is not a star. The light we see from
the Moon is reflected sunlight. Reflected light is important in other
ways. Reflectors on a bicycle bounce light from car headlights so
drivers can see the bicycle.

Unusual Sources of Natural Light

Many animals and plants can make their own light. This is called
bioluminescence (buy-oh-loo-muh-NESS-ens). You may have seen a
firefly at night. Fireflies produce light at the ends of their bodies. They
flash the light to communicate with other fireflies. Some mushrooms can
make their own light. If you walk in the forest in the dark, you may see
some. Most of the animals that make light live in the oceans and seas.
One example is the Anglerfish. This fish has a long, thin fin that grows
out of the top of its head. The tip of the fin gives off light to attract prey.

Light Is Important

Both natural and artificial light are very important. Light from the Sun is
needed for plants to grow. This light also helps keep animals and people
healthy. Most things people do require light. We do many activities during
daylight. We can also do many things at night because of artificial light.
Think about how different your life would be if we only had light from the Sun.

"Sources of Light"—Think About It!

1. Write the following sources of light in the correct column of the chart below.

- neon lights
- falling meteors
- lightning
- Northern lights
- sparklers
- traffic lights
- fireflies
- kerosene lamps

Natural Light Sources	Artificial Light Sources	

2. Fireflies and some algae make their own light. Is that light natural or artificial? Explain your thinking.

_____

_____

_____

3. What is one advantage of sunlight compared to a lightbulb? What is one advantage of a lightbulb?

_____

_____

_____

4. How would your life be different if you had no artificial light?

_____

_____

_____

Light and Energy

Light is a form of energy. It comes from the Sun. Light that we can see is called visible light. Light travels in waves from the Sun. Visible light is only one part of a family of waves that scientists call electromagnetic energy. Our eyes can see the waves of visible light, but cannot see the other waves of energy. They are invisible to our eyes. Below is a diagram of the electromagnetic spectrum that shows the different families of waves. You can see that visible light is a very small part of this spectrum.

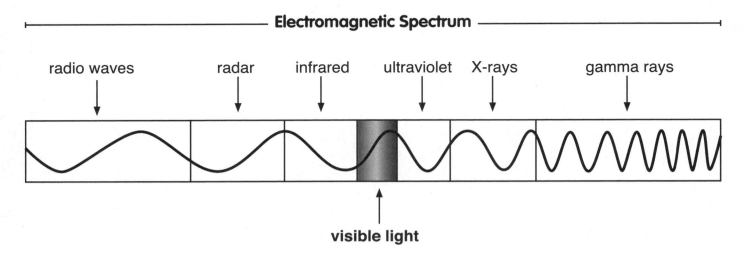

Visible Light and Color

Visible light from the Sun looks like white light. This light is made up of colors that mix together to make white light. White light can be split up to form a spectrum of its colors. A rainbow shows the spectrum of colors of visible light. The seven colors in visible light are violet, indigo, blue, green, yellow, orange, and red. Whenever visible light is split, these colors appear in the same order. Some scientists think that indigo and violet are the same color. They say there are only six colors in the spectrum.

People with normal vision can see all the colors of visible light in the spectrum. Some people have color blindness. This means they have difficulty seeing certain colors such as red and green. Dogs, cats, mice, and rabbits have poor color vision. They see mostly grays and some blues and yellows. Bees and butterflies have super color vision. They can even see some ultraviolet parts of the spectrum.

"Light and Energy"—Think About It!

1. How is all light energy the same? How is it different?

_____

_____

_____

_____

2. How can you tell that radio waves and infrared light exist if you cannot see them?

_____

_____

_____

_____

3. X-rays are one type of light energy. How are X-rays useful to doctors?

_____

_____

_____

_____

4. Imagine that the only colors you could see were black, white, and shades of gray. A dark-red book and a dark-green book would both look dark gray to you. What everyday activities would be difficult for you to do? Give at least three examples.

_____

_____

_____

_____

_____

Experiment: Make Your Own Rainbow

Create a rainbow to show the spectrum of colors of visible light.

What You Need

- A set of crayons or colored pencils
- A flashlight (one that has a narrow beam of light works best)
- A large bowl of water
- A mirror that will fit in the bottom of the bowl.

What You Do

1. Place the bowl of water near a blank wall.
2. Put the mirror in the bowl.
3. Shine the flashlight at the mirror.
4. Move the flashlight from side to side and up and down until you can see a rainbow on the wall or on the ceiling.
5. Use crayons or colored pencils to draw a picture of what you see on the back of this paper.

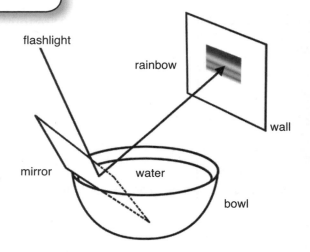

Think About It!

1. Write the colors in the order they appeared in the rainbow.

_____

_____

2. Is the light from the flashlight the same as white light from the Sun? How do you know?

_____

_____

_____

3. Where else can you see the spectrum of colors in visible light?

_____

_____

Experiment: How Does Light Travel?

Light travels in a straight line, and it travels fast—about 184,411 mi/s (300,000 km/s). One way you can tell that light travels in a straight line is shadows. If you stand with your back to the Sun, your body will block the light. So the shadow you see in front of you is the space where no light is getting through. Here is another way to check that light travels in a straight line.

What You Need

- A flashlight
- Some flour in a cup
- Newspaper
- A partner

What You Do

1. Spread the newspaper on top of a table.
2. Turn the lights off in the room.
3. Turn on your flashlight and point the light across the table.
4. Have your partner sprinkle the flour slowly in front of the light. Sprinkle the flour about 4 in (10 cm) from the lit end of the flashlight. Notice what happens.

Think About It!

1. How does this experiment show that light travels in a straight line?

_____

_____

_____

_____

_____

_____

_____

_____

Reflected Light

We can see light from things that produce light, such as the Sun and fire. But how do we see objects that do not produce light? Light travels in a straight line and it bounces off objects. Light that bounces off an object is called reflected light. Moonlight is reflected sunlight. Light from reflective clothing is light that bounces off the clothing. Reflected light also travels in a straight line.

How do we see objects? Light from a light source reflects off an object. Then the reflected light travels in a straight line into our eyes. We cannot see objects when it is completely dark because there is no light to reflect off them.

Think About It!

1. Label the following diagrams with these words: light source, object, reflected light, light, eye.

2. You go into a dark room. At first, you cannot see anything. Slowly you begin to see the outlines of objects in the room. Is there any light in the room? How do you know?

_____

_____

_____

_____

_____

_____

Experiment: Refracted Light

Light slows down when it travels from air into a liquid. If light travels from air straight into water, it slows down but keeps moving in a straight line. If light enters water at an angle, it slows down and changes direction. This change in direction is called refraction. After light changes direction, it keeps moving in a straight line. The same thing happens when light travels through solid material such as glass. Try the experiment below to see refraction for yourself.

What You Need

- A clear glass half-filled with water
- A pencil

What You Do

1. Put the pencil in the water so it leans against one side of the glass.
2. Look at the pencil from above. Look at the pencil from the side.

Think About It!

1. What does the pencil look like from above? What does the pencil look like from the side?

_____

_____

_____

_____

_____

2. Where does the pencil seem to break? Why does this happen?

_____

_____

_____

_____

_____

Experiment: Light Passing Through Materials

What materials will light pass through? Try this experiment to find out.

What You Need

- A clear plastic or glass cup
- A piece of wax paper
- A piece of tissue paper
- A piece of construction paper
- A piece of aluminum foil
- A flashlight

What You Do

1. Read all the steps to understand what you will do. Before you do the next steps, write your predictions in the chart below.
2. Place the objects in front of a wall. Shine the flashlight onto each of the objects. (Do one object at a time.)
3. Observe what happens.
4. Does the light pass through any of the objects? How much light passes through? Record your observations.

Object	Prediction: What will happen?	Result: What happened?
Clear plastic or glass cup		
Wax paper		
Tissue paper		
Construction paper		
Aluminum foil		

"Experiment: Light Passing Through Materials"—Think About It!

1. Will light pass through the clear cup if you put water in it? Why or why not?

_____

_____

_____

2. Put water in the cup to check your prediction. What happened to the light?

_____

_____

_____

3. How could you stop all sunlight from coming though windows?

_____

_____

_____

4. Will a clear object, such as a sheet of glass, make a shadow? Why or why not?

_____

_____

_____

5. People sometimes put frosted glass in a window. Frosted glass lets in some light, but people cannot see through it. Give at least two reasons people might use frosted glass in a window.

_____

_____

_____

_____

What Can You See Through?

Transparent Objects

When you look through a clear glass window, you can see what is on the other side. This happens because light can pass right through the glass. Another way to say this is that clear glass transmits light. Materials or objects that transmit light are called transparent.

Translucent Objects

What happens when you look through a frosted glass window? You can see a little bit through the window, but you cannot clearly see what is on the other side. This happens because only a small amount of light is transmitted through the glass. Materials or objects that transmit only a little light are called translucent.

Opaque Objects

Can you see through a wooden door? No, the door does not let any light through. The wood absorbs the light instead of transmitting it. Materials or objects that absorb light are called opaque.

Think About It!

1. In the chart below, list examples of materials and objects that are transparent, translucent, and opaque. List at least three examples in each column.

Transparent	Translucent	Opaque

Light Technology

The Sun was the first light source used by people. Later in history, people started to burn fuels to make light. First they burned animal fat in hollow objects. Over time, people designed new containers for burning fats. They added wicks to make the fire in the lamps burn more evenly. They started to use other fuels such as olive oil, beeswax, fish oil, whale oil, and nut oils. In the 1700s and 1800s, new lamps were designed. These used fuels that came from the ground, such as kerosene and coal. But the world was still a dark place for many people. Good fuels and lamps were expensive. Gas street lamps lit up only the area around each lamp.

Lightbulbs Today

Today most lighting depends on electricity. These are some different light sources used in homes, schools, and stores.

Incandescent: Inside these lightbulbs is a thin wire that is heated by electricity. When the wire gets very hot, it gives off a visible light. It also gives off a lot of wasted heat. Incandescent bulbs do not last very long. They also use a lot of electricity to produce a bright light. These bulbs are not expensive.

Halogen: Halogen lightbulbs work in the same way as incandescent bulbs. A wire inside the bulb is heated to produce light. The light from halogen bulbs is much brighter than the light from incandescent bulbs. Halogen bulbs also last longer, but they are more expensive. They also get very hot. They give off a lot of wasted heat.

Fluorescent: These are tubes filled with gas. Some bulbs are long, straight tubes, and others are spiral tubes. When electricity passes through the tubes, ultraviolet light is produced. This ultraviolet light causes other chemicals in the bulb to give off visible light. Fluorescent bulbs are more expensive than incandescent bulbs, but they use less electricity. They also give off much less heat.

Light-emitting Diode (LED): These are very different from other lights because they have a special material inside. The material produces light when electricity passes through the bulb. Different colors of light can be produced with different materials. LED lights last a very long time. They use very little electricity and do not get hot. LED lights are very expensive.

"Light Technology"—Think About It!

1. Street lights provide light at night. Lights are also used in parks, playing fields, and many other places. What is one advantage of having these lights? What is one disadvantage of having these lights?

_____

_____

_____

_____

_____

2. In the web below, summarize important points about each type of lighting.

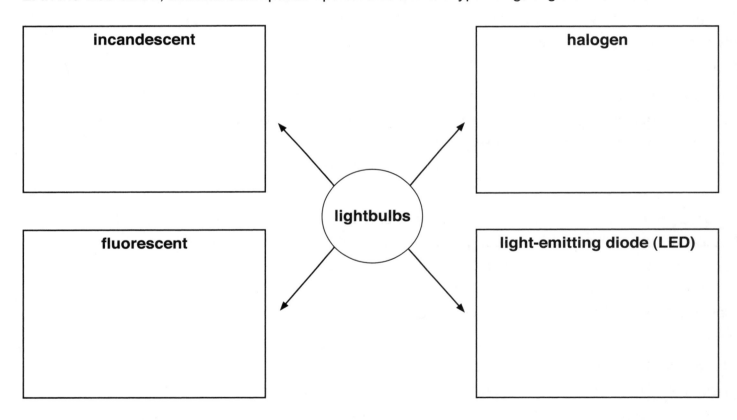

3. Which light or lights do you think are the best for your home? Why?

_____

_____

_____

Experiment: What Is Sound?

Light is a form of energy. Sound is also a form of energy. Sound is energy that can be heard. Sound is made when energy causes an object to vibrate, or move back and forth very quickly. Sometimes you can also feel sound vibrations. You make sound when the vocal cords in your throat vibrate. Try this experiment to feel the vibrations of sound.

What You Need

- A cardboard tube
- Paper
- Tape

What You Do

1. Tape the paper over one end of the tube.

2. Sing or speak into the other end of the tube.

3. As you sing or speak, gently touch the paper at the end of the tube.

Think About It!

1. What did you feel when you touched the paper? _____

_____

_____

2. Where else might you feel sound vibrations? _____

_____

_____

Sound Waves

In the activity above, your vocal cords made vibrations. How did the vibrations move from your vocal cords to the end of the tube? Sound travels in waves, which are like the waves in an ocean. Like ocean waves, sound waves go up and down. Each vibration makes one wave. Sound energy travels from place to place in sound waves. Sound waves are stronger or louder near the source of the sound because the waves have more energy there. The sound gets weaker or softer farther away from the source because the energy gets used up.

Experiments: Traveling Sound (Experiment 1)

Sound waves need to travel through something. Can sound waves travel through a gas, a liquid, and a solid? Try the following experiments to find out.

What You Need

- A wooden table
- A partner

What You Do

1. Work with a partner. Stand by the table. Have your partner tap lightly on the top of the table.
2. In your notebook, describe what you hear.
3. Put one ear on the table and hold a hand over your other ear. Have your partner tap again.
4. In your notebook, describe what you hear.

Experiment 1—Think About It!

1. Can sound travel through a gas, such as air? How do you know? _____

_____

_____

_____

2. Can sound travel though a solid, such as a table? How do you know? _____

_____

_____

3. Describe the difference in the sound you heard when you were standing by the table and when you had your ear on the table.

_____

_____

_____

_____

58

Experiments: Traveling Sound (Experiment 2)

What You Need

- A bowl or bucket
- Two metal spoons
- Water
- A partner

What You Do

1. Fill the bowl or bucket with water.
2. Stand by the bowl. Have your partner tap the two spoons together under the water.
3. In your notebook, describe what you hear.
4. Place one ear on the bowl, and hold a hand over your other ear. Have your partner tap the spoons again. In your notebook, describe what you hear.

Experiment 2—Think About It!

4. Can sound travel through a liquid, such as water? How do you know? _____

_____

_____

5. Describe the difference in the sound you heard when you were standing by the bowl and when you had your ear on the bowl. _____

_____

_____

6. Could a swimmer who is underwater hear a boat that was on the water? Why or why not?

_____

_____

Sound Facts

- Sound travels fastest through solids and slowest through gases.
- Lightning and thunder happen at the same time. Light travels faster than sound.
  If the lightning is far away, we see the lightning before we hear the thunder.

Changing How Sound Travels

Reflected Sound

Have you ever heard an echo? An echo is sound reflecting, or bouncing off, a surface. Light will reflect off a mirror. Sound will reflect off a surface, too. Sound will keep bouncing around until it loses its energy.

Some animals use sound in a special way. Bats and whales send out sounds that bounce off surfaces. The echoes tell them where the objects are. Using sound in this way is called echolocation.

Absorbed Sound

Can you stop sound from traveling far? Can you stop sound from reflecting? Can you make sound quieter? Materials that are not smooth or hard can help you do these things.

Have you ever been in an empty house that no one lives in? You probably noticed a lot of echoes. Soft materials absorb sound. They stop echoes. An empty house has no soft materials to absorb the sound. Adding carpets, furniture, and drapes helps quiet the sound.

Think About It!

1. Would hard or soft materials be best for a room in which you watch television or listen to music? Why?

_____

_____

_____

2. Many large concert halls contain some hard materials and some soft materials. Why do you think they do?

_____

_____

_____

Experiments: Loudness and Pitch

Experiment 1: Loudness

Sounds can be soft or loud. A sound will be louder when you are closer to the source. Sound will be softer when you are farther away. The loudness of a sound also depends on the size of the vibration. Large vibrations make loud sounds. Smaller vibrations make softer sounds. Try this experiment.

What You Need

- 2 elastic bands the same size, one thick and one thin; large enough to stretch around a shoe box
- A shoe box without a lid

What You Do

1. Place the elastic bands around the box so they go over the opening. Leave some space between the two elastic bands.
2. Pluck each elastic by lifting it up about 0.5 in (1 cm) and letting go. Compare the sound made by each band. Answer questions 1 and 2 below.
3. Lift one elastic band 0.5 in (1 cm), let go, and listen to the sound. Lift the same elastic band 1 in (2.5 cm), then 1.5 in (4 cm).

Experiment 1—Think About It!

1. Which elastic band made the loudest sound? _____

2. What does your answer to question 1 tell you about the vibrations made by each elastic band?

_____

_____

3. How did the sound of the elastic band change when you stretched it more?

_____

4. When did the elastic band make the largest vibrations? Was it when you lifted it 0.5 in (1 cm) or 1.5 in (4 cm)

_____

continued next page ☞

Experiment 2: Pitch

When you say a sound is high or low, you are talking about the pitch of the sound. A sound's pitch depends on how many vibrations, or sound waves, happen in a second. Sounds with a high pitch have more vibrations each second than sounds with a low pitch. Try this experiment.

What You Need
- A ruler
- A desk or table

What You Do

1. Hold the ruler against the desktop or tabletop with one hand. Position the ruler so that most of it is off the desk. Pluck the ruler. Watch and listen.
2. Hold the ruler so that most of it is on the desk. Pluck the ruler. Watch and listen.

Experiment 2—Think About It!

1. What differences did you see and hear? _____

_____

_____

_____

_____

2. Which position of the ruler caused more vibrations? How do you know?

_____

_____

_____

_____

_____

_____

Hearing Sounds

We hear with our ears. Our ears are special organs that pick up vibrations made by sound. The ear is made up of three different sections: the outer ear, the middle ear, and the inner ear. These parts all work together with our brain so we can hear and understand sounds.

Most animals have ears that help them hear sounds. Animal ears come in many shapes and sizes. Most of the time, ears are found on an animal's head. Some animals have hearing organs that do not look like ears. For example, crickets have small, pale spots on their front legs that sense sound. Snakes do not have an outer ear, but they do have an inner ear. Snakes also feel vibrations through the ground. These vibrations travel through a snake's lower jaw, and into the inner ear.

Measuring Volume

Sounds can be loud or soft. This is called the volume of sound. Sounds that have more energy are louder. Sounds with less energy are softer. Decibels (dB) are used to measure how much energy is in sound. If you have good hearing, the softest sound you can hear is 0 dB. One of the loudest sounds ever heard was the eruption of a volcano in 1883. Scientists estimate that the sound was 180 dB. People 1,864 mi (3,000 km) away from the volcano heard the eruption.

Measuring Hearing Range

People and animals can hear a range of sounds, from low-pitched sounds to high-pitched sounds. The pitch of sounds is measured in Hertz (Hz). One vibration per second is one Hertz. Low-pitched sounds have lower values of Hertz. High-pitched sounds have higher values of Hertz.

People can hear sounds that range from 20 Hz to 20,000 Hz. Dogs can hear sounds that range from 40 Hz to 45,000 Hz. This means that dogs can hear sounds at a higher pitch than people can. Have you ever heard a dog whistle? The whistle makes a sound with a pitch that is too high for you to hear, but dogs can hear it.

This chart shows the lowest-pitched and highest-pitched sounds that people and various animals can hear.

Animal	Range of Hearing in Hz
People	20 to 20,000
Dogs	40 to 45,000
Cats	45 to 65,000
Bats	2,000 to 120,000
Blue Whales	5 to 120,000
Giraffes	5 to 120,000
Mice	2,300 to 85,000
Tuna	50 to 1,100

"Hearing Sounds"—Think About It!

1. Rank the following sounds from softest to loudest. Write each sound where you think it belongs in the chart.

   - normal conversation
   - a whisper
   - loud thunder
   - car horn
   - power lawn mower
   - vacuum cleaner

Sound	Decibels
	20 dB
	50 dB
	70 dB
	100 dB
	110 dB
	120 dB

2. Scientists sometimes disagree on the hearing range of some animals. Why do you think this happens?

_____

_____

_____

_____

3. Which animals can hear sounds that are lower in pitch than sounds people can hear?

_____

_____

_____

_____

4. Can bats and tuna hear the same sounds? How do you know?

_____

_____

_____

_____

The History of Hearing Aids

Some people find that they do not hear as well as they used to. This problem is called hearing loss. Many people over the age of 60 have hearing loss, but sometimes younger people have to cope with this problem.

Throughout history, scientists and inventors have developed different types of hearing aids to help people hear better. Let's take a look at how hearing aids have changed over time.

The Ear Trumpet

One of the first hearing aids was called an ear trumpet. It was a tube that was narrow at one end and wide at the other end. A person put the narrow end against one ear, and people spoke into the wide end.

Ear trumpet

Ear trumpets started to become popular in the late 1700s. People were still using them in the early 1900s. Ear trumpets did help people hear a little better, but new inventions that worked much better would soon come along.

Electronic Hearing Aids

The first electronic hearing aids were invented at the beginning of the 1900s. They were large boxes that weighed several pounds, with an earpiece that was connected to the box by a wire. These hearing aids were too large and heavy for people to carry around with them.

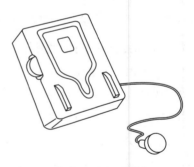

Electronic hearing aid from the early 1950s

In the 1950s, scientists created much smaller hearing aids that could fit in a shirt pocket. These hearing aids still used a wire to connect the box to the earpiece. Before long, scientists invented hearing aids small enough to fit behind the ear. The invention of very small batteries helped make behind-the-ear hearing aids possible.

Behind-the-ear hearing aid from the 1960s

continued next page

Digital Hearing Aids

The newest hearing aids use digital technology. That is the same technology used in computers and cell phones. Digital technology allowed scientists to create hearing aids that are small enough to fit inside the ear. Some hearing aids are small enough to fit deep inside the ear so they are almost impossible to see.

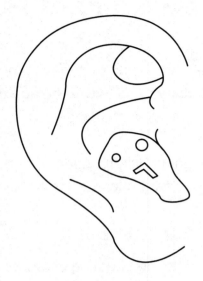

In-the-ear hearing aid

Today's digital hearing aids can do some remarkable things:

- **Adjust to changes in volume:** The hearing aid automatically adjusts itself so loud sounds are not made too loud, but soft sounds are made louder.

- **Adapt to background noise:** Imagine your friend is speaking to you in a crowded, noisy room. If your hearing aid makes your friend's voice *and* all the background noise louder, you might still have trouble hearing your friend. Today's hearing aids can make your friend's voice louder without making the background noise louder.

- **Help people with different types of hearing loss:** Some people have problems hearing low tones such as the sound of tuba, or high tones such as the sound of a flute. Today's hearing aids can be adjusted so they only make the tones louder that a person has trouble hearing.

"The History of Hearing Aids"—Think About It!

1. Look at the picture of the ear trumpet. How do you think this hearing aid got its name?

_____

_____

_____

_____

2. In the 1950s, scientists started created hearing aids that people could wear on their bodies. Why would this type of hearing aid be more useful than one with a large, heavy box?

_____

_____

_____

_____

3. Why do you think scientists invented hearing aids that fit deep inside the ear so they are almost impossible to see?

_____

_____

_____

_____

_____

4. There have been many improvements to the hearing aid. What invention that we use today would you like to improve? Tell one way that you would improve it.

_____

_____

_____

_____

Musical Instruments

Musical instruments produce many different sounds. How do they do this?

Winds

Some instruments make sounds when air is pushed through a tube. One example is the recorder. A recorder is a wind instrument. Wind instruments have many different shapes, but the main part of the instrument is a hollow tube. When air is blown into the hole at one end of the tube, a sound is made. A recorder has finger holes to change the pitch of the sound. Other wind instruments change pitch by changing the length of the tube. A trombone is one example.

recorder

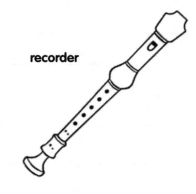

Strings

The sounds that string instruments make come from vibrating strings. Some examples of string instruments are the guitar, violin, and piano. String instruments make high and low sounds by using different lengths and thicknesses of string. The pitch of a string can be changed by making the string tighter or looser. String instruments can be played in many ways. They can be plucked like a guitar, played with a bow like a violin, or played by pressing keys like a piano.

violin

Percussion

Percussion instruments produce a sound when they are struck with something. Often percussion instruments provide the beat of the music. Bells and xylophones are percussion instruments that can play melodies. Drums are usually tuned so they play one note. They can be tuned to play different notes by tightening or loosening the top of the drum. Tighter tops produce higher notes. Bigger drums produce lower notes.

Some percussion instruments, such as maracas, are shaken to make sounds. Tambourines can be struck and shaken to make sounds.

drum

"Musical Instruments"—Think About It!

Try It!

Make a musical instrument. Work with two or three classmates. Talk about the type of musical instrument each of you could make—wind, string, or percussion. After you have made your instruments, see if you can play music together.

Here are materials you might use:

- shoe boxes
- elastic bands
- bottle caps
- uncooked beans, rice, or popcorn

- pieces of board
- tacks
- foil pie plates
- waxed paper

- glass jars
- string
- paper towel rolls
- tin cans with plastic lids

- fishing line
- bells
- wooden dowels

1. In the box below, draw a labeled diagram showing your finished instrument.

2. Describe how your instrument produces sound. _____

_____

_____

3. Can you change the pitch of the sound? How? _____

_____

_____

4. Could you improve the design of your instrument? How? _____

_____

_____

Safety with Light and Sound

Many devices apply the properties of light and sound. Many of these devices make our lives safer. For example,

- UV-coated sunglasses protect our eyes from harmful sunlight.
- Safety sensors stop doors from closing on something in the way.
- Back-up signals on trucks and cars warn us the vehicle is moving.
- Ear plugs protect our ears from loud noises.

Some technologies that use light and sound have disadvantages. For example, talking on a cell phone can be dangerous while walking, biking, or driving. Loud sounds can damage your hearing. Loud sounds can come from music, motors, and nature.

Think About It!

1. Lights help us see better at night. But some people think we have too many lights at night. Why do you think some people feel this way?

   _____

   _____

2. People can enjoy music with stereos and portable music players. How could these devices be dangerous?

   _____

   _____

3. What new light or sound device would you like to see invented? What would the device do? What problems might happen because of the device?

   _____

   _____

   _____

   _____

   _____

Light and Sound Vocabulary

You have learned many words while studying light and sound. From the list below, choose words to complete the sentences. Use each word only once. Not all the words will be used. Share your sentences with a partner. Be ready to defend your choices.

artificial	**bioluminescence**	**spectrum**	**LED**
halogen	**Hertz**	**pitch**	**refracted**
reflected	**transparent**	**translucent**	**absorb**
decibels	**vibrations**	**volume**	

1. A frosted window is _____.

2. A pencil in a glass of water looks broken because the light is _____ by the water.

3. When people speak, they produce _____ with their vocal cords.

4. An echo is _____ sound.

5. _____ lightbulbs are very bright, but they get very hot.

6. A glow stick is an example of _____ light.

7. White light is made up of a _____ of colors.

8. Soft materials help _____ sound in a room.

9. We measure how loud or soft a sound is in _____.

10. _____ depends on the number of vibrations per second.

Rocks and Minerals

What is the difference between rocks and minerals?

A mineral is made of only one substance. It is not a mixture of different substances. A rock is made from a mixture of two or more minerals.

You can think of minerals as different colors of modeling clay. Each color of clay represents a different mineral. So if you have three balls of clay—one green, one blue, and one red—each ball would be a different mineral. Now imagine that you take a chunk from each ball of clay, press them together, then roll the clay into a ball. This ball would represent a rock because it is made of a combination of minerals.

Granite is a common type of rock. You have probably seen it before. If you look closely at a piece of granite, you will see flecks of different colors. These different colors come from the minerals that make up granite. The minerals in granite are feldspar, quartz, and mica.

Why are some rocks all one color, unlike granite?

Even rocks that are all one color contain two or more different minerals. Think back to the ball of modeling clay made from three different colors. You can still see the green, blue, and red clay used to make the ball. But if you mix the clay for a long time, eventually it will all become brownish-gray. The colors mix with each other. In rocks that are all one color, the minerals have mixed together, so you do not see the different colors.

What do minerals look like?

Minerals do not all look the same. They can be different colors and shapes. Some minerals sparkle and some are dull. Some minerals, such as quartz, form in crystals. Other minerals are metals. Gold and silver are two minerals that are metals. The names of these minerals also tell you what color they are.

quartz

continued next page

Which is harder—rocks or minerals?

This is a trick question! Some rocks and minerals are hard, and some are soft. Granite is a hard rock that is a great material to use for countertops because it is not easy to scratch or chip. Other rocks, such as sandstone, are much softer. Artists sometimes use sandstone for their sculptures because it is easy to carve. Some minerals are soft enough to scratch with your fingernail. Diamond is a mineral and it is the hardest substance found in nature.

Do I have rocks in my head?

If you do not already, you probably will soon. Rocks are a very interesting subject to learn about, and so are minerals. You may even become a rock collector. If that happens, you may end up with rocks all over the place—in your desk, in your pocket, and in the box where you keep your collection. And you will have many thoughts about rocks in your head.

"Rocks and Minerals"—Think About It!

You probably know more about rocks and minerals than you realize. Use what you know, and your brain power, to answer these questions.

1. Unpaved roads are often covered with gravel, which is small chunks of rock. What are two reasons gravel might be used on roads?

_____

_____

_____

_____

_____

_____

_____

"Rocks and Minerals"—Think About It! (continued)

2. Gemstones such as rubies and emeralds are used to make jewelry. Rubies and emeralds are both minerals. What are two characteristics of these minerals that people find beautiful?

_____

_____

_____

_____

_____

_____

3. Some buildings—especially old buildings—are made from blocks of rock. Give one advantage and one disadvantage of building with blocks of rock.

_____

_____

_____

_____

_____

_____

4. Most types of glass are made from silica, or sand. Sand is made up of tiny pieces of many types of minerals and rocks. List at least eight glass objects commonly found in homes. (The objects may include other materials.)

_____

_____

_____

_____

_____

_____

Three Types of Rock

All rocks can be grouped into one of three categories. The categories are based on how they were formed.

Igneous rock is formed when magma (hot liquid rock beneath Earth's surface) cools and becomes solid. Some igneous rock cools and becomes solid beneath Earth's surface. Other igneous rock cools and becomes solid on Earth's surface. Granite and obsidian are igneous rocks.

granite

Sedimentary rock is formed from sediment, which is tiny pieces of other rocks. The sediment settles in layers at the bottom of a lake or ocean. As more and more sediment builds up, the weight of the sediment at the top pushes down on the sediment at the bottom. The pressure from all this weight squeezes together the sediment and turns it in to sedimentary rock. Limestone and sandstone are sedimentary rocks.

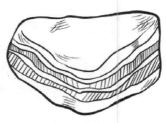

sandstone

Metamorphic rock is made from sedimentary or igneous rock that has been changed by pressure, or heat, or both. Pressure might come from the shifting of Earth's crust. The heat from magma might "bake" nearby rocks, changing them into metamorphic rocks. Most metamorphic rocks are formed deep within Earth. Marble and slate are metamorphic rocks.

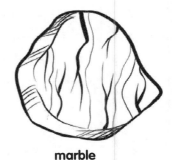

marble

Think About It!

1. Tina found a rock that has stripes. She thinks the stripes are different layers. What type of rock do you think she has—igneous, sedimentary, or metamorphic? Tell why you think so.

_____

_____

_____

_____

_____

The Rock Cycle

Did you know that Earth constantly recycles rock? Here is how this can happen:

> Red hot magma inside Earth is pushed to the surface. (When magma flows out of a volcano, it is called lava.) The magma cools to form igneous rock.

> Rocks on Earth's surface are broken down into tiny pieces by wind and water. Over time, the sediment is carried to a lake or ocean. There, it settles in layers on the bottom. Eventually, the sediment becomes sedimentary rock.

> Heat and pressure turns sedimentary rock into metamorphic rock. For example, when huge plates of Earth's crust shift position, they produce a lot of heat. This melts the rock into magma.

Think About It!

1. Roger found a shiny black rock when hiking near a volcano. The rock reminds him of glass, but light does not shine through it. To which category of rock do you think it belongs? Why?

_____

_____

_____

_____

_____

_____

_____

"The Rock Cycle"—Think About It! (continued)

2. Create a diagram to help you remember the stages of the rock cycle. Use illustrations, key words, or both.

Rock Cycle Activity

Perform this activity as a class to see how the rock cycle works. Before you start, review the rock cycle. Then read the questions on the next page and answer them during the activity.

What You Need

- 3 or 4 crayons of different colors
- A crayon sharpener or a regular table knife
- A piece of aluminum foil 8 in by 12 in (20 cm by 30 cm)
- Several heavy books
- A candle and matches
- A clothespin
- A dish of cold water (optional)

What You Do

1. Fold the aluminum foil in half lengthwise and flatten the crease.

2. Use the crayon sharpener or a table knife to create crayon shavings. Let the shavings drop onto the middle of the aluminum foil. Create a pile of shavings that is about 2 in by 2 in (6 cm by 6 cm) and 0.5 in to 1 in (1 cm to 2 cm) thick.

3. Fold the aluminum foil over the shavings. Fold the edges so no shavings can fall out.

4. Place the foil packet on a book and place one or two heavy books on top of it. Wait 2 to 3 minutes.

5. Carefully open the packet and observe what changes have taken place.

6. Wrap the crayon material in the foil as before. Add one or two more heavy books. Have two or three students take turns increasing the pressure by pushing down on the books.

7. Open the packet and observe any changes.

8. Rewrap the crayon in the foil and make sure all edges are carefully folded.

9. Use a clothespin to hold the foil packet over a lit candle for 2 to 3 minutes to melt the crayon. Let the packet cool. (Put it in a dish of cold water to make it cool faster.)

10. Open the packet. Observe any changes.

SAFETY ALERT

Be sure your teacher or another adult does **Step 9**.

"Rock Cycle Activity"—Think About It!

After Step 2

1. Remember that this activity helps you understand the rock cycle.

a) What do the crayons represent?

_____

_____

_____

_____

b) What do the shavings represent?

_____

_____

_____

_____

2. The crayon shavings form a pile on the foil. Which part of the rock cycle does this represent?

_____

_____

_____

_____

After Step 4

3. The heavy books create pressure. They push down on the crayon shavings. What do the heavy books represent?

_____

_____

_____

_____

_____

After Step 5

4. What type of "rock" has been created? _____

After Step 7

5. A new type of "rock" has been created. What type of rock is it?

_____

_____

After Step 9

6. Heat makes the "rock" inside the foil melt. In the rock cycle, what is this melted rock called?

_____

After Step 10

7. What type of "rock" has been created? _____

8. What would happen next in the rock cycle?

_____

_____

_____

_____

_____

_____

_____

_____

_____

_____

Identifying Minerals

Geologists are scientists who study the structure of
Earth. How do they identify minerals? They compare
properties, or characteristics, of the minerals. Here are a
few of the properties geologists look at when identifying
minerals.

rock hammer

Color

Looking at the color of a mineral can be helpful. Some
minerals can be many colors. Quartz can be clear,
purple, yellow, green, brown, or pink. Malachite is
always green, but lots of minerals are green. Color is not
enough to identify a mineral sample.

Luster

How well does the mineral reflect light? Imagine
gold shining in the light. The shine is created by light
reflecting off the gold. Geologists have a list of words to
describe luster. For example, gold has a metallic luster
and quartz has a glassy luster. Turquoise has a waxy
luster, like the way light reflects off a candle.

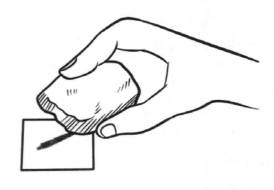

streak plate

Streak

If you rub a mineral across an unglazed piece of
porcelain, it leaves a line of powder. This line of powder
is the streak. The piece of porcelain is called the streak
plate. A mineral's streak is always the same color.
Quartz always leaves a white streak, even if the quartz
is clear, purple, yellow, green, brown, or pink.

continued next page ☞

Transparency

Geologists observe how light passes through the sample. This tells geologists about the sample's transparency. Transparency has three basic categories:

- Transparent—You can see objects through the mineral.
- Translucent—Light passes through the mineral, but you cannot see objects through it.
- Opaque—No light passes through the mineral.

Hardness

Some minerals are very soft and easy to scratch. Other minerals are extremely hard and very difficult to scratch. Diamond is the hardest mineral on Earth. To test the hardness of a mineral, geologists use the Mohs' Hardness Scale. This is named after Friedrich Mohs, who invented the scale. Mohs rated the hardness of some well-known minerals on a scale of 1 to 10, with 10 being the hardest.

The minerals in the scale can be used to test the hardness of a sample. Geologists use each mineral to scratch the sample. Only a mineral that is harder than the sample will scratch it. For example, topaz will scratch quartz. Feldspar will not scratch quartz. If topaz scratches the sample, they know the sample is not harder than topaz. This helps narrow down the choices.

Scientific reference books give the properties of many types of minerals. A geologist can look up the properties to identify a sample.

Mohs' Hardness Scale
1 Talc
2 Gypsum
3 Calcite
4 Fluorite
5 Apatite
6 Feldspar
7 Quartz
8 Topaz
9 Corundum
10 Diamond

"Identifying Minerals"—Think About It!

1. Abdul scratches a mineral sample with a piece of quartz.

a) What property of the sample is he investigating? _____

2. Susan holds a mineral sample up to a light. The light shines through, but she cannot see anything through the sample.

a) What property of the mineral is Susan investigating? _____

b) What word would she use to describe the sample? _____

3. Kwame has two mineral samples that look similar. He is not sure if both are the same mineral. He rubs them across an unglazed porcelain tile. The marks they leave are different colors.

a) What property of the minerals is he investigating? _____

b) Could his two samples both be the same mineral? How do you know?

_____

_____

_____

_____

4. Tom holds a mineral sample under a light. He notices that the sample shines like metal.

a) What property of the mineral is he investigating? _____

b) What word would he use to describe how light reflects off the sample?

_____

5. Why is looking at color alone *not* a good way to identify a mineral sample?

_____

_____

_____

_____

Pros and Cons of Mining

Mining for Minerals

Rocks that contain minerals are called ore. Mining is the process of digging to find ore. If the ore is close to the surface, miners can create an open-pit mine. First they scrape away the soil on the surface to get to the ore underneath. Then they use explosives such as dynamite, or special power tools, to break the ore into chunks. The ore is sent to a place called a refinery, where people separate the useful minerals from the rock.

If the ore is far below the surface, miners create an underground mine by digging tunnels. Miners travel down an elevator and work in different tunnels to break up the ore in the tunnel walls. Then the ore is brought up to the surface and sent to a refinery.

We need mines because we need to have minerals. We use minerals to make things such as toothpaste, medicine, and airplanes. But mines also create problems. Read about some of the pros (advantages) and cons (disadvantages) of mining.

The Pros of Mining

Here are some of the advantages of mining for minerals:

- **Useful Products:** Minerals are in many of the products we use every day, including cars, computers, cell phones, and televisions. Can you imagine what it would be like to live without these conveniences?
- **Jobs:** Mining provides jobs. People who work in refineries would also lose their jobs if mining stopped. Many mines are in places where there are few other jobs.
- **Exports:** American mines produce more minerals than we need. Mining companies can sell the extra minerals to other countries. This brings money into the United States and helps provide jobs.
- **New Technology:** New devices and ideas make mining safer. They make mining more efficient, too. Other workplaces might also use these devices and ideas.

continued next page

The Cons of Mining

Here are some of the disadvantages of mining for minerals:

- **Danger to Miners:** Working in mines can be dangerous. Miners can be trapped underground if a tunnel collapses. Miners breathe dangerous gases and rock dust in the mine that can make them very sick.
- **Harming the Environment:** Mining can put dangerous pollution into the environment. Mines can destroy habitats that animals rely on to survive. Some mining companies try to repair the habitat. Damage to animal populations might be permanent.
- **Abandoned Mines:** When all the minerals have been dug out of a mine, the mine may be abandoned. Abandoned mines are dangerous places for curious people to explore.

"Pros and Cons of Mining"—Think About It!

Use this story to answer the questions.

Tara lives in a small town in the northern part of her state. The town had just a few residents until several years ago. Then a mine opened just outside of town. Now more than 1,000 people live in her town. Many of them work in the mine. Just last week, the newspaper said that the mine will close next year.

Tell how the following people might feel about the closing of the mine. Explain your thinking.

1. Miners and their families: _____

_____

_____

_____

_____

_____

_____

_____

_____

2. People concerned about the environment: _____

_____

_____

_____

_____

_____

_____

_____

3. Owners of local stores and restaurants: _____

_____

_____

_____

_____

_____

_____

4. People who work to protect animal populations: _____

_____

_____

_____

_____

_____

_____

Minerals in Your Home

Many building materials are made from minerals. Take a look at some common examples.

Bricks and Ceramic Tiles

Clay minerals are used to make bricks and tiles. Wet clay is easy to shape. Once it has been baked, it is very strong. Clay is also a good insulator. Clay helps to keep out the cold in winter and the heat in summer.

Mortar

Bricklayers spread mortar between bricks. Mortar holds the bricks together. Mortar contains clay minerals and other minerals such as gypsum. Mortar is sticky when wet and it sticks to the bricks. When mortar dries, it adds strength to brick walls. Mortar also helps keep out water.

Drywall

Drywall is large panels used to build walls inside homes. Another name for drywall is gypsum board. The mineral gypsum is the main ingredient in drywall.

To make drywall, water and gypsum are mixed into paste. The paste is sandwiched between two long sheets of paper. After the paste hardens, the drywall is baked to make it even stronger. Then the drywall is cut into panels. Gypsum will not catch fire easily. Drywall adds strength and safety to a building.

Electrical Wiring

The mineral copper is used to make electrical wiring. Electricity flows easily through copper. Copper wire bends without breaking.

In the past, water pipes in homes were usually made of copper. But copper is now much too expensive to use for pipes. Plumbing in newer homes is made from less expensive materials.

Kitchen and Bathroom Taps

Your kitchen and bathroom taps are probably a silver color. They are coated with a metal called chromium, which is often called chrome. Chromium comes from the mineral chromite. Chromium does not rust easily so it is a good material to use in wet places.

Minerals in Your Home Quiz

Many of the products used at home are made from minerals.

Match each product with a mineral in it. In the table, the properties of each mineral will give you clues.

Did You Know?

- A television contains over 30 different minerals.
- A telephone contains over 40 different minerals.

Mineral	Properties
Mica	• Can be ground into a powder • Reflects light
Quartz	• Hard and transparent • Liquids cannot pass through it
Halite	• Dissolves in water • Tastes like salt
Corundum	• Very hard • Can be ground into small particles with rough edges
Talc	• Very soft and breaks up easily • Absorbs liquids
Clay minerals	• Mixes well with liquids • Grainy, scratchy texture
Graphite	• Quite soft • Makes a black streak when rubbed against something

1. Emery boards are used for filing fingernails. Mineral: _____

2. Powder that helps keep things dry. Mineral: _____

3. Clear flower vases hold water. Mineral: _____

4. Pencils make marks that we can erase. Mineral: _____

5. Kitchen salt adds flavor to food. Mineral: _____

6. Stovetop cleaners remove dried spills that can be tough to get off.

Mineral: _____

7. Some makeup sparkles. Mineral: _____

How Minerals Make Fossils

Read on to find out how minerals make fossils, and why we are able to find fossils on Earth's surface.

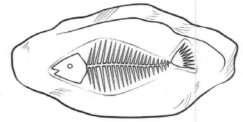

Step 1 An animal dies. The animal's body sinks to the bottom of the water. The soft parts of the animal's body rot away. Only the bones and teeth are left. The skeleton is slowly buried by sediment.

Step 2 More and more layers of sediment build up over the skeleton. The weight of these layers turns the sediment to rock. This takes thousands of years.

Step 3 Water slowly dissolves the bones of the animal's skeleton. This leaves a hole or cavity in the rock that is the same shape as the skeleton.

Step 4 Minerals in the water slowly build up inside the hole. Eventually, these minerals fill the hole, making the same shape as the skeleton. A fossil has been formed.

Step 5 How do people find fossil's on Earth's surface if fossils form deep underground? Natural events, such as an earthquake or the making of mountains, push the fossil up to the surface. Over time, wind and water wear away the rock. The fossil is now visible.

Fossil Facts

- Fossils are formed in sedimentary rock. Layers of sediment make up sedimentary rock. These same layers bury a skeleton so it can become a fossil.
- The oldest known fossils were formed about 3.5 billion years ago.
- Plants can also become fossils.
- Fossils tell us about animals that became extinct a long time ago.
- Some fossils show traces that animals left behind. Eggs, nests, footprints, and even animal droppings can become fossils.

Make Your Own Fossil

With a few simple materials, you can see for yourself how fossils are made.

What You Need

- Modeling clay
- A small object to "fossilize," such as a seashell
- Petroleum jelly

What You Do

Make a mold for the fossil

1. Create two small, thick slabs of modeling clay. Each slab should be a bit thicker than the object you are going to fossilize.

2. Cover the object you want to fossilize with petroleum jelly. This will stop the clay from sticking to the object.

3. Lay the object on one of the clay slabs. Push it into the clay, but do not push it right to the bottom of the slab. Part of the object can stay above the surface of the slab.

4. Put the other clay slab on top of the first slab. Push down on the top slab to make sure it surrounds the object.

5. Lift off the top slab of clay. Carefully lift the object out of the bottom slab. Try not to stretch the bottom slab as you remove the object.

6. Leave the two slabs in the open until they are dry. The dents your object made in the slabs are the mold for your fossil.

Make the fossil

7. Cover both sides of the mold with petroleum jelly.

8. Create a ball from soft modeling clay and put it in one side of the mold.

9. Put the other side of the mold on top and carefully press down. This makes the ball take the same shape as the mold.

10. Slowly open the mold and carefully remove the fossil you have made. Leave the fossil in the open to dry.

"How Minerals Make Fossils/Make Your Own Fossil"—Think About It!

Review the information in "How Minerals Make Fossils" and the instructions for the activity "Make Your Own Fossil." Complete the chart below to compare the activity to the way real fossils are made.

In the Activity	When Real Fossils Are Formed
1. A mold is made by pressing an object between two slabs of clay.	
2. A ball of clay is pressed between the two sides of the mold.	
3. The fossil is "discovered" by opening the mold.	

Did You Know?

The Dinosaur National Monument is a great place to see dinosaur fossils. This park is located in the Uinta Mountains on the border between Colorado and Utah. Do an Internet search for "Dinosaur National Monument." Look for information about the park and learn about the fossils found there.

Rocks and Minerals Crossword

Use your knowledge of rocks and minerals to complete the crossword puzzle.

Across

3. Unlike a rock, this is made of only one substance
6. The hardest substance found in nature, with a hardness of 10 on Mohs' Hardness Scale
7. Hot, liquid rock found beneath Earth's surface
8. A mineral used to make electrical wiring
10. Magma that has been pushed out of a volcano
11. The category for rocks that have been changed by heat, or pressure, or both
12. The line of powder left behind when a mineral is rubbed against a surface
13. A mineral used to make drywall for construction

Down

1. The material that settles at the bottom of a lake or ocean and eventually turns into rock
2. A property of minerals that is related to how light passes through them
4. The category for rocks formed by magma that has cooled
5. The word used to describe a mineral that no light passes through
9. A mineral that adds flavor to foods you eat

STEM-Related Occupations

To learn more about some of these occupations visit the following websites:

www.sciencebuddies.org/science-engineering-careers

https://kids.usa.gov/watch-videos/index.shtml

Accountant
Aerospace Engineer
Agricultural Engineer
Agricultural Technician
Aircraft Mechanic and
   Service Technician
Animal Breeder
Animal Trainer
Animator
Anthropologist
Architect
Astronaut
Astronomer
Athletic Trainer
Audio Engineer
Audiologist
Automotive Mechanic
Biochemical Engineer
Biochemist/Biophysicist
Biologist
Biology Teacher
Biomedical Engineer
Business Owner
Cardiovascular Technician
Carpenter
Chef
Chemical Engineer
Chemical Technician
Chemistry Teacher
Chiropractor
Civil Engineer
Civil Engineering Technician
Climate Change Analyst
Clinical Psychologist
Computer Engineer
Computer Programmer
Computer Systems Analyst
Construction Manager
Counselling Psychologist
Dietetic Technician

Dietitian and Nutritionist
Doctor
Electrical Engineering Technician
Electrician
Electronics Engineer
Emergency Medical Technician
Environmental Engineer
Environmental Engineering Technician
Environmental Restoration Planner
Environmental Scientist
Epidemiologist
Fire-Prevention Engineer
Fish and Game Worker
Food Science Technician
Food Scientist and Technologist
Forest and Conservation Technician
Forest and Conservation Worker
Geoscientist
Graphic Designer
Hydrologist
Industrial Engineer
Interior Designer
Landscape Architect
Manufacturing Engineer
Marine Architect
Marine Biologist
Math Teacher
Mechanical Engineer
Mechanical Engineering Technician
Medical Lab Technician
Medical Scientist
Meteorologist
Microbiologist
Microsystems Engineer
Mining and Geological Engineer
Molecular and Cellular Biologist
Neurologist
Nuclear Engineer
Nursery and Greenhouse Manager
Nutritionist

Occupational Health and Safety Specialist
Optical Engineer
Optometrist
Paleontologist
Patent Lawyer
Pathologist
Park Ranger
Petroleum Engineer
Pharmacist
Physical Therapist
Physician
Physician Assistant
Physicist
Pilot
Psychologist
Registered Nurse
Respiratory Therapist
Robotics Engineer
Robotics Technician
School Psychologist
Seismologist
Software Developer (Applications)
Software Developer (Systems Software)
Soil and Plant Scientist
Soil and Water Conservationist
Space Scientist
Speech-Language Pathologist
Statistician
Transportation Engineer
Transportation Planner
Urban Planner
Veterinarian
Video Game Designer
Volcanologist
Water/Wastewater Engineer
Wind Energy Engineer
X-ray Technician
Zookeeper
Zoologist
Wildlife Biologist

Science, Technology, Engineering, and Mathematics (STEM) Occupation Brochure

Create a brochure about a STEM-related occupation.

STEP 1: Plan Your Brochure

❑ Fold a piece of paper the same way your brochure will be folded.
Before writing the brochure, plan the layout in pencil. Sections
of the brochure should include
  • Job description
  • Training or degree needed
  • Work environment
  • How the occupation relates to STEM
  • Interesting facts

❑ Write the heading for each section where you would like it to be in the brochure.

❑ Plan where graphics or pictures will be placed in the brochure.

STEP 2: Complete a Draft

❑ Research information for each section of your brochure. Check your facts.

❑ Read your draft for meaning, then add, delete, or change words to make your writing better.

❑ Plan what illustrations or graphics you will put into your brochure.

STEP 3: Checklist

❑ My brochure is neat and well organized.

❑ My brochure has accurate information.

❑ My brochure has pictures or graphics that go well with the information.

❑ I checked the spelling.

❑ I checked the punctuation.

❑ My brochure is attractive.

What Does a Pharmacist Do?

Pharmacists work with medicines. If you are sick, the doctor might want you to take a special type of medicine called a prescription medicine. People can buy prescription medicines only if their doctor has given permission. Prescription medicines are sold at a drug store.

Pharmacists work in drug stores. They are experts in different types of medicines. They have learned how each type of medicine helps people get better.

Pharmacists make sure you get the right amount of the prescription medicine your doctor wants you to take. They put a label on the medicine to tell you how much to take and how often to take it.

Sometimes, a pharmacist has to make medicines. For example, a pharmacist might make a cream to spread on a rash. The doctor will tell the pharmacist what to put in the cream.

Drug stores also sell medicines that are not prescription medicines. People do not need a doctor's permission to buy this type of medicine. A pharmacist can help people choose the best medicine to help them feel better.

Pharmacists also help people stay safe when they are taking medicine. For example, a pharmacist might say, "This medicine might make you sleepy. Do not drive a car after taking this medicine."

Not all pharmacists work in drug stores. Some work in hospitals, and some work in nursing homes.

"What Does a Pharmacist Do?"—Think About It!

1. What do people need before they can buy a prescription medicine?

_____

_____

_____

2. It can be dangerous to take too much of a medicine or to take it too often. How do pharmacists help to make sure people take prescription medicines correctly?

_____

_____

_____

_____

3. Tell an example in the text that shows how a doctor and a pharmacist might work together.

_____

_____

_____

_____

_____

4. Frank has a cough, but he does not feel sick enough to go to a doctor. How could a pharmacist help Frank?

_____

_____

_____

5. Why is it a good idea for hospitals to have pharmacists?

_____

_____

_____

Air Traffic Controllers

Traffic lights tell cars when to stop and when to go. Roads are divided into lanes so cars going in opposite directions do not crash into each other. Traffic lights and lanes on roads are just two ways that we control road traffic to help avoid accidents.

At any moment in time, there are thousands of airplanes flying over North America. There are no traffic lights in the air, and no roads with lanes. How do planes avoid flying into each other? Air traffic controllers (ATCs) help with that important job. An ATC gives instructions to pilots to make sure that planes do not crash into each other.

ATCs are involved in all three main parts of a flight:

Three Main Parts of a Flight

Preflight and Takeoff	En Route	Approach and Landing

continued next page ☞

1. **Preflight and takeoff:** An ATC tells pilots when it is safe to move the plane to the runway and when it is safe to take off. This prevents accidents between planes that are moving on the ground at an airport. It also prevents accidents between planes that are taking off and planes that are landing.

2. **En route:** "En route" (sounds like "on root") is French for "on the way." During this part of the flight, the airplane climbs to its cruising altitude, which is the height at which it flies for most of the journey. ATCs use radar to watch the plane and other planes flying in the same area. What if two planes look as though they might fly into each other? An ATC will warn the pilots and give instructions to avoid an accident. For example, an ATC might tell one plane to fly higher until the other plane has passed.

3. **Approach and landing:** When the destination airport is near, the pilot brings the plane closer to the ground. During the approach, the pilot lines up the plane with the runway where it will land. An ATC tells the pilot when it is safe to begin the approach and land the plane. If another plane is about to land on the same runway, the ATC will tell the pilot to circle around the airport. Once the other plane has landed and moved off the runway, an ATC will tell the pilot who is circling that it is safe to begin the approach and land.

Characteristics of Air Traffic Controllers

It takes a special person to be an ATC. Here are some of the characteristics that ATCs need to have:

- **Ability to stay calm in stressful situations:** ATCs need to stay calm so they can think clearly and quickly when dealing with dangerous situations.
- **Excellent health:** Being an ATC can be very stressful. An ATC needs a healthy body that can handle the stress. People need to go through a thorough medical exam before they can become an ATC.
- **Ability to focus:** A disaster could happen if an ATC loses concentration and begins to daydream. ATCs need to be able to stay focused for long periods of time.
- **Good decision-making skills:** Airplanes fly at very high speeds. When a dangerous situation develops in the air, the ATC might have only a few seconds to decide how to avoid an accident.

Thanks to the hard work of ATCs, flying in an airplane is safer than travelling in a car.

"Air Traffic Controllers"—Think About It!

1. In the second paragraph, why did the writer include "(ATCs)" after the words "air traffic controllers"?

_____

_____

_____

_____

2. During which part of a flight is the airplane flying highest in the sky? Where in the text did you find the answer?

_____

_____

_____

_____

3. Write two questions you would like to ask an air traffic controller.

_____

_____

_____

_____

4. Would you want to become an air traffic controller? Why or why not?

_____

_____

_____

_____

What Does an Architect Do?

Architects are people who plan new buildings. Before construction workers can start a building, they need to have a plan to follow.

The first thing an architect does is talk to the person who wants the building. That person is called the client. The architect finds out what type of building the client wants. Will it be a house, a store, an office building, a hospital, a sports arena, a shopping mall, or a school?

Next, the architect finds out what needs to be inside the building. For a house, the architect needs to know what rooms are needed. For example, how many bedrooms and bathrooms are needed?

The architect might make some quick sketches to show ideas for the building. Some sketches show what the outside of the building will look like. Other sketches show where each room will be and how big it will be. The client looks at the sketches and might ask for changes. Then the architect makes new sketches showing the changes the client asked for.

When architects design a building, they make sure
- The building is safe for people to use.
- The building meets the needs it was designed for.
- The building has a pleasing appearance.

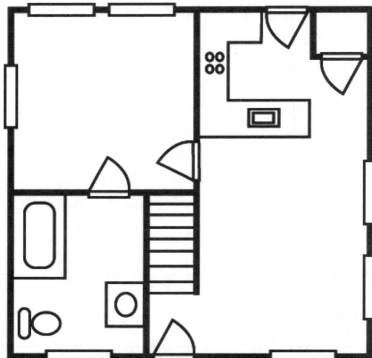

An architect's plan showing a single floor of a house.

Brain Stretch

Visit the following website to check out famous structures and buildings from around the world.

www.sciencekids.co.nz/pictures/structures.html

"What Does an Architect Do?"—Think About It!

1. Why does an architect need to plan a building before construction can start?

_____

_____

_____

2. What are two things an architect needs to find out before starting to plan a building?

_____

_____

_____

_____

3. Why do architects need to be able to draw?

_____

_____

_____

4. Would you like to become an architect? Explain your thinking.

_____

_____

_____

_____

5. An architect planning a school will ask, "About how many students will be in each classroom?" Why does the architect need this information?

_____

_____

_____

_____

What Does an Engineer Do?

You have probably heard the word "engineer" before. Have you ever wondered what an engineer does?

An engineer is a person who plans, or designs, structures. There are many different types of structures, so there are many different types of engineers. The chart below gives just a few examples.

Type of Engineer	Examples of Structures the Engineer Works On
Structural engineer	Houses, sports arenas, hospitals, bridges
Aerospace engineer	Airplanes, helicopters, rockets, spacecraft
Computer engineer	Desktop computers, laptop computers, modems
Automotive engineer	Cars, buses, trucks

How does an engineer design a structure? Many engineers work through the following steps:

Step 1: Identify challenges or problems
With every structure, there are challenges or problems to be solved. For example, one challenge of building a sports arena is to make it strong enough to hold up the weight of thousands of people who have come to see a football game.

Step 2: Brainstorm solutions
Engineers try to come up with different and imaginative ways of solving problems. Then they decide which ideas are worth investigating further.

Step 3: Explore possible solutions
Engineers think carefully about the best solutions they came up with. They consider the advantages and disadvantages of each solution. Then they decide which solution will work best.

Step 4: Build a model or prototype
A model is often a small version of the structure. For example, an engineer might build a model of a sports arena that fits on a tabletop. A prototype is often a full-size version of the structure. Engineers who are designing a new car build a working prototype of the car. Models and prototypes show the solutions engineers came up with to solve problems.

continued next page ☞

This model shows part of a bridge that will cross a highway.

Step 5: Improve the model or prototype

Engineers always try to make their structures even better. They look at the model or prototype they have created and try to find ways to improve it. Eventually, they come up with a final design.

Becoming an Engineer

Do you have what it takes to become an engineer? Below are some of the characteristics of a good engineer.

- **Curious:** Engineers like to figure out how things are built, how they work, and how they could be improved.

- **Creative:** The best engineers are good at coming up with creative ways to solve problems.

- **Interested in math and science:** Engineers take university courses in math and science as part of their education.

- **Works well with others:** Engineers usually work as part of a team. They need to be able to get along with others and communicate their ideas clearly.

"What Does an Engineer Do?"—Think About It!

1. Write the type of engineer who would work on the following structure.

    a) motorcycle _____

    b) space station _____

    c) shopping mall _____

    d) tablet computer _____

2. Select one of the structures from the chart on page 102 or choose another structure. Explain one way that you would try to improve the structure if you were an engineer.

_____

_____

_____

_____

3. Look back at the steps engineers work through. Explain how you might use, or how you have used, two of these steps in school.

_____

_____

_____

_____

4. Give two reasons why it is important to have engineers in our world.

_____

_____

_____

_____

How Engineers Help Us Every Day

Engineers are people who build all types of things that make our world work better. Many of the things you see and use every day were created by engineers. Some engineers work with chemicals to create new textiles, more flexible plastics, and stronger building materials. Others work in cities to build roads, bridges, and skyscrapers. Some engineers make medical supplies for hospitals, technology for space travel, and find new and safer ways to clean up the environment. Engineers can build or create just about anything!

List 10 things engineers build or do to make people's lives easier.

1._____
_____

2._____
_____

3._____
_____

4._____
_____

5._____
_____

6._____
_____

7._____
_____

8._____
_____

9._____
_____

10._____
_____

continued next page ☞

Imagine and design a device that will help make people's lives easier. Make sure to label your device.

Describe your device on a separate piece of paper. Explain your thinking about why your device would be helpful to people and how the device would work.

Technology Collage

Look through magazines and newspapers to find examples of technology. Cut and paste the examples into a collage below. On a separate piece of paper, write about how technology is used in people's lives. Include how you use technology in your daily life.

Think Like an Engineer!

An engineer is a person who designs and build things. Engineers want to understand how and why things work. Engineers try different ideas, learn from their mistakes, then try again. Engineers call these steps the design process.

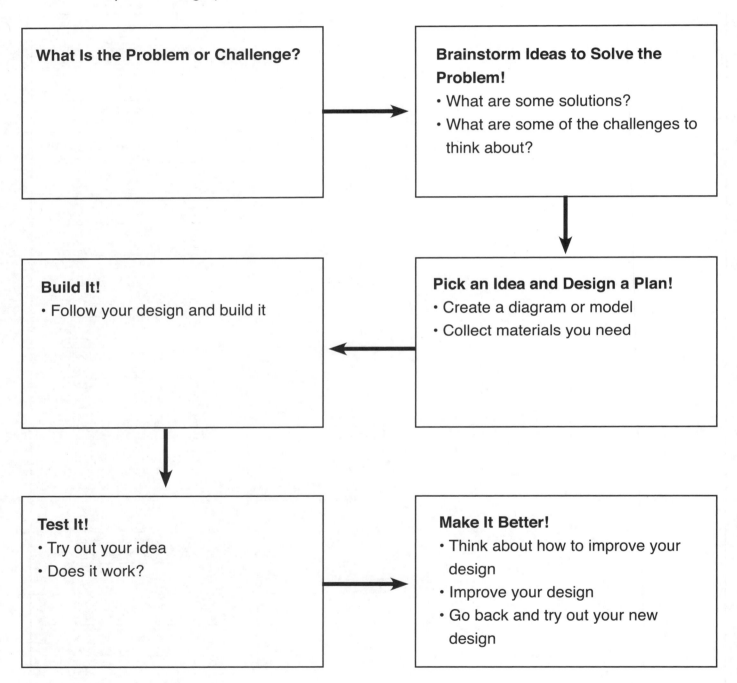

What Is the Problem or Challenge?

Brainstorm Ideas to Solve the Problem!
• What are some solutions?
• What are some of the challenges to think about?

Build It!
• Follow your design and build it

Pick an Idea and Design a Plan!
• Create a diagram or model
• Collect materials you need

Test It!
• Try out your idea
• Does it work?

Make It Better!
• Think about how to improve your design
• Improve your design
• Go back and try out your new design

Remember to be patient. Take your time to figure things out.

The Design Process

1. What is the problem or challenge?

_____

_____

_____

2. Think about it! What are some ideas to solve the problem or challenge?

_____

_____

_____

_____

_____

_____

_____

_____

continued next page ☞

3. Pick a design idea! Draw and label a picture of your design. Write about your plan.

_____

_____

continued next page 👉

4. Get ready! What materials do you need?

continued next page ☞

5. Test it! Build your design and try it out.

Did it work?   Yes ☐   A little ☐   No ☐

6. Make it better! How can you make your design better?

_____

_____

_____

7. Try your design out again! What happened?

_____

_____

_____

8. What do you wonder about?

_____

_____

9. What are you proud of?

_____

_____

STEM Rubric

	Level 1 Below Expectations	Level 2 Approaches Expectations	Level 3 Meets Expectations	Level 4 Exceeds Expectations
Knowledge of STEM Concepts	• Displays little understanding of concepts. • Rarely gives complete explanations. • Intensive teacher support is needed.	• Displays a satisfactory understanding of most concepts. • Sometimes gives appropriate, but incomplete explanations. • Teacher support is sometimes needed.	• Displays a considerable understanding of most concepts. • Usually gives complete or nearly complete explanations. • Infrequent teacher support is needed.	• Displays a thorough understanding of all or almost all concepts. • Consistently gives appropriate and complete explanations independently. • No teacher support is needed.
Application of STEM Concepts	• Relates STEM concepts to outside world with extensive teacher prompts. • Application of concepts rarely appropriate and accurate.	• Relates STEM concepts to outside world with some teacher prompts. • Application of concepts sometimes appropriate and accurate.	• Relates STEM concepts to outside world with few teacher prompts. • Application of concepts usually appropriate and accurate.	• Relates STEM concepts to outside world independently. • Application of concepts almost always appropriate and accurate.
Written Communication of Ideas	• Expresses ideas with limited critical thinking skills. • Few ideas are well organized and effective.	• Expresses ideas with some critical thinking skills. • Some ideas are well organized and effective.	• Expresses ideas with considerable critical thinking skills. • Most ideas are well organized and effective.	• Expresses ideas with in-depth critical thinking skills. • Ideas are well organized and effective.
Oral Communication of Ideas	• Rarely uses correct STEM terminology when discussing STEM concepts.	• Sometimes uses correct STEM terminology when discussing STEM concepts.	• Usually uses correct STEM terminology when discussing STEM concepts.	• Consistently uses correct STEM terminology when discussing STEM concepts.

Notes: _____

_____

_____

STEM Focus _____

Student's Name	Knowledge of STEM Concepts	Application of STEM Concepts	Written Communication of Ideas	Oral Communication Skills	Overall Grade

STEM Expert!

_____

Fantastic work!

Great Work!

_____

Keep up the effort!

Unit: Habitats and Communities

Habitats, pages 2–3
1. No. The nest provides shelter but does not provide food, water, or space to hunt or to find a mate.
2. Yes, because it could provide the food, water, air, light, and space plants and animals need to survive.
3. It is important for animals to find a mate so they can reproduce and raise a family.
4. A lake or stream is a good habitat for a beaver because it provides mud that beavers need to build homes and the water to build it in. The forest around the lake or stream provides the logs and branches needed for the home and food.

Different Types of Habitats, pages 4–6
1. Raccoon habitat: city. Raccoons hunt for food in garbage cans, and a city is a place where garbage cans are available as a food supply.
2. Coral habitat: ocean. If scuba divers have to be careful of coral, then coral must live in an underwater habitat.
3. Alligator habitat: wetland. A wetland provides swampy areas and places to hunt both water and land animals.
4. Badger habitat: prairie. Badgers hunt ground squirrels, which live in prairie habitats.

Animal Adaptations, pages 7–9
1. Answers may vary. Sample answers—Birds: Feathers help them to fly and keep them warm in cold weather so they can survive in colder climates; Giraffes: Their long neck allows them to eat leaves on high branches, which means less competition for food; Beavers: Their wide, flat tail helps them swim and steer better, and balance when moving branches. It also serves as an alarm; Snakes: Their jaws spread wide so they can swallow larger prey, which means they do not have to eat as often and can go longer between meals. Students may also suggest other animal adaptations, such as birds with specialized beaks for cracking seeds or picking bugs out of bark, or animals with sharp claws for catching prey easier.
2. Sample answers: Swimming: Duck—webbed feet; Fish—fins; Seal—flippers
3. Sample answers: Hunting: Owl—wings for flying, sharp claws, excellent eyesight; Rattlesnake—venom; Shark—sharp teeth
4. Sample answers: Hiding: Polar bear—white fur for hiding in snow; Chameleon—ability to change color; Turtle—shell color same as habitat

Humans and Habitats, pages 10–11
Answers may vary. Sample answers:
1. I feel happy, because the plan will provide more space to build houses, which means my business can survive.
2. I feel unhappy, because many plants will be destroyed when the forest is cut down. Animals who live in the forest will lose their habitat and may die if they cannot find a new place to live.
3. I feel happy, because I can buy one of the new houses.

Habitat Communities, pages 12–13
1. A habitat community and a school community are similar because the members of both a habitat community and my school community are together in one place and the members depend on one another to meet their needs.
2. Animals and plants are equally important in a habitat community because they depend on each other to survive. For example, many animals need plants for food or shelter, and animals can help plant species survive by helping to spread seeds.
3. Illustrations should include two labeled examples of animals and plants depending on each other. Have students share and discuss their illustrations with a partner or small group.

Food Chains, pages 14–15
1. Sunlight is important because it provides the energy that starts the food chain.
2. If all the grasshoppers disappeared, then the frogs would not have enough to eat. Also, more grass would survive since there would be no grasshoppers to eat it, and hunting would be more difficult for the other animals. Eventually each animal in the chain would die from lack of food.
3. sunlight → plant → rabbit → fox
4. sunlight → algae → shrimp → fish → seal → polar bear

Producers, Consumers, and Decomposers, pages 16–17
1. Butterfly. A butterfly is not a producer because only plants are producers.
2. Decomposers are important because they break down dead plants and animals into tiny pieces that living plants can use to make food.
3. Sunlight—neither P nor C; Plants—P; Deer—C; Wolf—C
4. If there were no decomposers, plants would not have enough tiny pieces of dead things to make food with. This means there would be fewer plants for consumers to eat and they would eventually starve.
5. a) False b) False

What Is for Dinner? pages 18–19
1. Herbivore: butterfly, deer, giraffe; Omnivore: chimpanzee, pig, raccoon; Carnivore: dolphin, shark, snake
2. Humans are omnivores by nature, though some may choose to be herbivores (vegetarians).
3. a) Carnivorous b) herbivore c) omnivorous d) herbivorous

Natural Habitats and Humans, pages 20–21
1. No, a farm is not a natural habitat because farms are created by humans.
2. Recycling paper helps save forests because when paper products are recycled, new trees do not need to be cut down to provide the paper. Trees are an important part of forest habitats, so cutting down fewer trees in forests helps to save forest habitats.
3. Drawings will vary. Confirm that students have illustrated a natural habitat.

Generalist and Specialist Animals and Plants, page 22
1. a) specialist b) generalist
2. Specialist plants and animals will be affected most by changes in a habitat because the habitat may no longer be able to meet their special needs.

Habitat Word Search, page 23
1. habitat 2. adaptation 3. community 4. chain
5. decomposer 6. carnivore

Unit: Pulleys and Gears

What Is a Pulley? pages 24–25
1. Up 2. Down
3. The advantages of a compound pulley are change of direction in the force and less force is needed to lift the load.
4. Answers will vary.

Experiment: Make a Simple Pulley, page 26
1. It is a fixed pulley since the broom handle is attached to the chairs and does not move.

Experiment: Make a Movable Pulley, page 27
1. The paper clip moved up. The paper clip is a movable pulley. When I pulled on the string, it pulled the paper clip pulley up.
2. Sample answer: Use a stronger string and paper clip. Attach the string to the table more securely.

What Is a Gear? pages 28–29
1. a) Gear 1: counter-clockwise; Gear 2: clockwise; Gear 4: clockwise; Gear 5: counter-clockwise. b) Gear 1: clockwise; Gear 2: counter-clockwise; Gear 3: clockwise
2. The large gear will turn slower, because the larger gear has twice as many teeth as the smaller gear, so the smaller gear has to make two full turns to every one full turn of the larger gear.
3. The large gear will turn 1.5 times. Since the large gear has twice the number of teeth as the small gear, the small gear moves twice the speed of the large gear, and the large gear moves at half the speed of the small gear. Half the speed means half the number of turns; One-half of 3 turns is 1.5 turns.

Pulleys and Gears in Daily Life, page 30
1. Two pulleys are needed, because both ends of the clothesline needs to move.
2. A clothes dryer needs pulleys and gears to turn the drum where the clothes are put.
3. A flagpole uses a pulley to raise the flag much higher than a person can reach.

Opposite Directions, pages 31–32
1. a) Counter-clockwise, because the belt between pulley A and pulley B is crossed. b) Clockwise. Since the belt between pulley D and pulley A is not crossed, both pulleys rotate in the same direction.
2. a) Gears A and E would move in the same direction, and the two neighboring gears cannot move in the same direction. b) Add or remove a gear.

Changing Direction: Bevel Gears, pages 33–34
1. wind 2. vertically 3. horizontally
4. Wind is the force that makes the top grinding stone turn.
5. vertical, horizontal
6. Bevel gears are used in a windmill, because they can change the direction of motion.

Changing Direction: Worm Gears, page 35
1. A person turning the knob is the force moving the hands.
2. A worm gear. A spur gear cannot turn a worm gear, so the worm gear must be the first step.
3. Yes. If the first bevel gear is turned horizontally, the gears will change horizontal motion into vertical motion which will turn the clock hands.
4. The horizontal motion of turning the knob is changed into the vertical motion of the hands around the clock face.

Changing Direction: Rack and Pinion, page 36
1. The pinion moves the rack, pulling the buckle tighter.
2. The hand or muscle is the force that makes the gears move.
3. The handle is the pinion. The bar is the rack.
4. The pinion would turn clockwise and counter-clockwise.

Bicycle Gears, pages 37–38
1. The lowest speed (largest diameter gear) is best for riding uphill, because you do not need to pedal as hard to turn the gears.
2. The highest speed (smallest diameter gear) is better for a flat road because the gear turns several times for each turn of the pedal.
3. No, the pedalling motion is the same as the motion of the tires: vertical and circular. Yes, the gears can increase the force applied by the pedals (the tire rotates faster than the pedals in high speed, and slower than the pedals in low speed).
4. The front wheel is the output component because it is moved by the input component (the pedals). I know because if you flip a tricycle upside down and turn the pedals, the back wheels will not move, but the front wheel will.

Pulleys at Work: Conveyor Belt, page 39
1. The conveyor belt saves the effort and time required to carry groceries to the end of the counter.
2. The pully will turn clockwise since two pulleys connected by a belt that is not crossed will turn in the same direction.

Gears at Work: Pencil Sharpener, page 40
1. The input component is the handle. The output component is the cutting wheels. The handle makes the cutting wheels turn.
2. No, both the handle and the cutting wheels turn vertically.

Pulleys and Gears Riddles, page 41
1. load 2. movable 3. teeth 4. worm 5. bevel 6. rack and pinion
7. the chain 8. pedals 9. Pulleys and gears make things move!

Two Ways to Save Energy, pages 42–43
Sample answers:
1. Mrs. Petrof could car pool, or she could get a more energy-efficient car in order to save energy.
2. If you are able to take the stairs, please do.

Unit: Light and Sound

Sources of Light, pages 44–45
1. Natural Light Sources: falling meteors, lightning, fireflies, Northern lights; Artificial Light Sources: neon lights, sparklers, traffic lights, kerosene lamps
2. The light from fireflies and algae is natural light since it is not made by humans.
3. Sample answer: Sunlight is free. A light bulb works anytime and anywhere, not just during daytime.
4. Sample answer: My life would be different without artificial light, because I would only be able to do things when the Sun was shining. I would not be able to do many things at night, by candlelight.

Light and Energy, pages 46–47
1. All light energy can come from the Sun. Different types of light energy can be used for different tasks. Only part of the Sun's light energy can be seen by humans.
2. Sample answer: Devices such as a radio can be used to sense radio waves. You can feel the heat of infrared light or take a picture of it with an infrared camera.
3. X-rays are useful because they can be used to take pictures of bones inside a body.
4. Sample answer: It would be difficult to tell the difference between red and green traffic lights, peppers, apples, or wires. I would not be able to watch 3-D movies. It would be difficult to whether if the colors of my clothing matched.

Experiment: Make Your Own Rainbow, page 48
1. red, orange, yellow, green, blue, indigo (optional), violet
2. Yes, the light is the same, because it contained all colors of the rainbow just like the Sun's light.
3. Sample answer: In a rainbow and in the image from a crystal sun catcher.

Experiment: How Does Light Travel? page 49
1. I can see a straight beam of light in the flour cloud.

Reflected Light, page 50
1. Labels: Sun is "light source"; arrow going to flower is "light"; flower is "object"; arrow leaving the flower is "reflected light"; the eye is "eye."
2. There must be light in the room because the objects are reflecting light. That is why I can see the outline.

Experiment: Refracted Light, page 51
1. Looking from above, the pencil seems to change direction at the surface of the water. Looking from the side, the pencil seems to be broken at the surface of the water.
2. The pencil seems to break at the surface of the water. Light changes direction (refracts) as it goes from air to water, so the light is reflected in a different direction.

Experiment: Light Passing Through Materials, pages 52–53
Predictions will vary but should show understanding that light travels in straight lines.
Expected Results: amount of light passing through clear plastic or glass cup—all; wax paper—most; tissue paper—some; construction paper—little; aluminum foil—none
1. Yes, light will pass through, because water is clear.
2. All light passed through.
3. Sample answer: I can block the sunlight by covering the windows with heavy curtains.
4. No, a clear object won't make a shadow because it does not block the light.
5. Sample answer: People might use frosted glass to reduce the glare of bright light or to provide privacy.

What Can You See Through? page 54
1. Sample answer: Transparent—eyeglass lenses, clear plastic wrap, house windows, air; Translucent—plastic milk jug, wax paper, stained glass window, nylon stockings; Opaque—cement, wood, stone, desk

Light Technology, pages 55–56
1. Sample answer: Advantage—Street lights make it safer to walk at night. Disadvantage—You cannot see many stars in the sky because the street lights are too bright.
2. Sample answer:
Incandescent— heated wire inside glows to make light, waste a lot of heat, use a lot of (costly) electricity, do not last long, cost little to buy

Halogen—heated wire inside glows to make light, very bright, last longer, get very hot so waste a lot of heat

Fluorescent—tubes filled with gas, tubes can be straight or bent, ultraviolet light and chemicals in tubes cause light, expensive to buy but use less electricity, give off little (wasted) heat

LED—substance inside makes light when electricity goes through it, different substances make different colors, last a long time, do not get hot (no wasted heat), expensive to buy but inexpensive to power
3. Answers will vary but should provide a reason. Sample answer: Fluorescent bulbs because they use less electricity, and we have a lot of lights in our house that are on a lot.

Experiment: What Is Sound? page 57
1. I felt vibrations.
2. Sample answer: I feel sound vibrations from an amplified speaker or earphones and on my throat when I talk.

Experiments: Traveling Sound, pages 58–59
Experiment 1
1. Yes, sound can travel through a gas, because I heard the tap when I was standing by the table.
2. Yes, sound can travel through a solid, because I heard the sound when my ear was on the table.

3. The sound was louder or deeper when my ear was on the table.

Experiment 2

4. Yes, sound can travel through a liquid, because I heard the sound of the spoons when I was standing by the bowl.
5. The sound was louder or deeper when my ear was on the bowl.
6. Yes, the swimmer could hear a boat, because the sound of the paddle or motor would travel through the water.

Changing How Sound Travels, page 60

1. Soft materials would be best, because they absorb sound, reducing the echo.
2. Sample answer: Soft materials help reduce echoes, and hard materials are needed to support the structure and to direct sound out to the audience.

Experiments: Loudness and Pitch, pages 61–62
Experiment 1

1. The thicker band.
2. The thicker band made larger vibrations. The thinner band made smaller vibrations.
3. The sound got louder as the band was stretched more.
4. The largest vibrations happened when I lifted it 1.5 in (4 cm).

Experiment 2

1. When most of the ruler was off the desk, the sound was lower and the ruler waved farther up and down. When most of the ruler was on the desk, the sound was higher and the ruler shook faster and a shorter distance.
2. The ruler vibrated more (shook faster) when it was mostly on the desk.

Hearing Sounds, pages 63–64

1. a whisper, 20 dB; normal conversation, 50 dB; vacuum cleaner, 70 dB; power lawn mower, 100 dB; car horn, 110 dB; loud thunder, 120 dB
2. Sample answer: Different individuals within any species can have different hearing abilities. Measuring an animal's hearing ability may rely on observation of their reactions to sounds, and those reactions may vary for individual animals.
3. Blue whales and giraffes can hear sounds lower in pitch than sounds people can hear.
4. No, bats and tuna can't hear some sounds, because the highest frequency tuna can hear is lower than the lowest frequency bats can hear.

The History of Hearing Aids, pages 65–67

1. The ear trumpet looks like a musical trumpet. Both are tubes that are wide at one end and narrow at the other end.
2. A hearing aid that people wear on their bodies can easily go wherever the person goes. A large, heavy hearing aid would be difficult to carry around.
3. Some people want to hide the fact that they have hearing loss and use a hearing aid.
4. Sample answer: I would make a cell phone with a battery that lasts much longer so you do not have to recharge it so often.

Musical Instruments, pages 68–69
Answers will vary depending on the musical instruments students choose to build.

Safety with Light and Sound, page 70

1. Sample answer: Light blocks the stars, disrupts animals that are awake at night, and may keep people awake. Bright lights create too much contrast, making shadows where danger can hide.
2. The music may block important warning signals such as the sound of a car horn or the siren of an emergency vehicle. If the volume is too high, it can damage hearing.
3. Answers will vary.

Light and Sound Vocabulary, page 71

1. translucent 2. refracted 3. vibrations 4. reflected 5. halogen 6. artificial 7. spectrum 8. absorb 9. decibels 10. pitch

Unit: Rocks and Minerals

Rocks and Minerals, pages 72–74

1. Sample answer: Gravel is used, because the rough texture improves traction, reduces icing, and lasts longer than dirt alone.
2. Sample answer: People like these gemstones for their color, transparency, and sparkle.
3. Sample answer: Advantages—durable, strong, beautiful, may be available locally; Disadvantages—weight, may not be available locally, very heavy to work with
4. Sample answer: windows, mirrors, clocks, watches, some television and computer screens, drinking glasses, bowls, vases, some eyeglasses, magnifying glasses, light bulbs, and picture glass.

Three Types of Rock, page 75

1. She has sedimentary rock, because they form from layers of sediment.

The Rock Cycle, pages 76–77

1. He has igneous rock, because it is formed from magma or lava, which comes from a volcano.
2. Answers will vary.

Rock Cycle Activity, pages 78–80

1. a) Rocks on Earth's surface. b) sediment
2. Sediment building up
3. Layers of sediment that push down on layers below.
4. sedimentary 5. metamorphic 6. magma 7. igneous
8. Wind and water would break down the igneous rock into tiny pieces that will become sediment at the bottom of a lake or ocean.

Identifying Minerals, pages 81–83

1. hardness
2. a) transparency b) translucent
3. a) streak b) No, because a mineral always leaves the same color of streak.
4. a) lustre b) metallic
5. Because some types of minerals can be different colors.

Pros and Cons of Mining, pages 84–86

1. Miners and their families will be unhappy because they will lose their jobs.
2. People concerned about the environment will be happy because mines can cause pollution.
3. Owners of local stores and restaurants will be unhappy because people who lose their mining jobs will not have money to spend and may move out of the town.
4. People who protect animal populations will be happy because there will be less habitat destruction and less noise and other pollution.

Minerals in Your Home/Minerals in Your Home Quiz, pages 87–88

1. corundum 2. talc 3. quartz 4. graphite 5. halite
6. clay minerals 7. mica

How Minerals Make Fossils/Make Your Own Fossil, pages 89–91

1. Sediments surround the skeleton that will become a fossil.
2. Minerals in the water slowly build up in the cavity left by the skeleton after it has dissolved. (The cavity is like the mold in the activity.)
3. The rock containing the fossil is worn away by wind and water, revealing the fossil.

Rocks and Minerals Crossword, page 92

Across: 3. mineral **6.** diamond **7.** magma **8.** copper **10.** lava
11. metamorphic **12.** streak **13.** gypsum

Down: 1. sediment **2.** transparency **4.** igneous **5.** opaque
9. halite

¹S		²T		³M	⁴I	N	E	R	A	L		⁵O
E		R			G							P
⁶D	I	A	M	O	N	D		⁷M	A	G	M	A
I		N			E							Q
M		S		⁸C	O	P	P	E	R			U
E		P			U				⁹H			E
N		A			S		¹⁰L	A	V	A		
T		R							A			
	¹¹M	E	T	A	M	O	R	P	H	I	C	
		N							I			
		C					¹²S	T	R	E	A	K
	¹³G	Y	P	S	U	M						

What Does a Pharmacist Do? pages 95–96

1. Before people can buy a prescription medicine, they must have permission from their doctor.
2. Pharmacists put a label on medicine to tell people how much to take and how often to take it to make sure people take prescription medicines correctly.
3. The doctor might tell the pharmacist what to put in a cream for a rash and the pharmacist will make the cream for you.
4. A pharmacist can help Frank chose the best medicine to help his cough.
5. Sample answer: A pharmacist can give hospital patients medicines they need when they are leaving the hospital.

Air Traffic Controllers, pages 97–99

1. The writer is showing that the letters "ATCs" stand for "air traffic controllers."

2. The airplane is flying highest in the sky during the en route part of the flight. The answer is shown in the diagram.
3. Sample answer: Why did you want to become an air traffic controller? What has been your scariest moment as an air traffic controller?
4. Sample answer: I would want to become an air traffic controller because I like airplanes and airports, and I would feel good about doing a job that helps keep airplanes and passengers safe.

What Does an Architect Do? pages 100–101

1. An architect needs to plan a building before construction so construction workers have a plan to follow.
2. An architect needs to find out what type of building the client wants and what needs to be inside the building (what rooms are needed).
3. Architects need to be able to draw so they can make quick sketches of their ideas for the client. They must also be able to make detailed drawings of their plan for builders to follow so they know exactly what to do and how big to build things.
4. Sample answer: I would like to become an architect because I like building things and it would be interesting to plan how buildings would look.
5. The architect needs this information to know how big to make the classrooms so there is enough room for all the students.

What Does an Engineer Do? pages 102–104

1. a) automotive engineer; b) aerospace engineer; c) structural engineer; d) computer engineer
2. Sample answer: I would design a bed that made it impossible to sleep too late in the morning. The bed would start shaking when it was time to get up, and it would keep shaking until you got out of bed.
3. Sample answer: I used Step 2 and Step 3 to come up with a title for a story I wrote. First I brainstormed different titles (Step 2). Then I decided which title was best by thinking about what happened in the story and which title would make people most interested in reading the story (Step 3).
4. Sample answer: Engineers make structures better because they find ways to improve them. We need engineers to design many of the structures that we use every day.

How Engineers Help Us Every Day, pages 105–106

Discuss as a class the list of 10 things engineers build or do. Ask students to share their ideas. Create a bulletin board display of students' device drawings and descriptions, or ask a few volunteers to share their devices and descriptions with the class.

Technology Collage, page 107

Create a bulletin board display of students' collages.